With the Naval Brigade in Natal: 1899-1900

C. R. N. Burne

Photo by Middlebrook, Durban.

TWENTY THOUSAND MEN ENCAMPED UNDER GENERAL BULLER.

WITH THE NAVAL BRIGADE IN NATAL

1899-1900

Journal of Active Service

KEPT DURING THE RELIEF OF LADYSMITH AND SUBSEQUENT OPERATIONS IN NORTHERN NATAL AND THE TRANSVAAL, UNDER GENERAL SIR REDVERS BULLER, V.C., G.C.B.

BY

LIEUTENANT BURNE, R.N.

1902

For the Army, our comrades and our friends,
the Navy has nothing but the deepest respect and admiration.

INTRODUCTION

This Journal, completed before leaving the front in October, 1900, does not assume to be more than a somewhat rough and unadorned record of my personal experiences during ten months of the South African (Boer) Campaign of 1899-1900 while in detached command of two 12-pounder guns of H.M.S. *Terrible* and H.M.S. *Tartar*. Having been asked by some of my friends to publish it, I am emboldened to do so, in the hope that the Journal may be of interest to those who read it, as giving some idea of work done by a Naval Brigade when landed for service at a most critical time. A few notes on Field Gunnery are appended with a view to give to others a few ideas which I picked up while serving with the guns on shore, after a previous experience as Gunnery Lieutenant in H.M.S *Thetis* and *Cambrian*.

For the photographs given I must record my thanks to Lieutenant Clutterbuck, R.N., Mr. Hollins, R.N., and other kind friends.

C.R.N.B.

April, 1902.

CONTENTS

CHAPTER I

Outbreak of the war—The Transport Service and despatch of Army Corps from Southampton—Departure of a Naval Brigade from England and landing at Capetown and Durban—I join H.M.S. *Philomel*

CHAPTER II

I depart for the front with a Q.-F. Battery from H.M.S. *Terrible*—Concentration of General Buller's army at Frere and Chieveley—Preliminary bombardment of the Boer lines at Colenso—The attack and defeat at Colenso—Christmas Day in camp

CHAPTER III

Life in Camp and Bombardment of the Boer lines at Colenso—General Buller moves his army, and by a flank march seizes "Bridle Drift" over the Tugela—The heavy Naval and Royal Artillery guns are placed in position—Sir Charles Warren crosses the Tugela with the 5th Division, and commences his flank attack

CHAPTER IV

Spion Kop and Vaal Krantz—General Buller withdraws the troops and moves once more on Colenso—We hold Springfield Bridge—Buller's successful attack on Hussar Hill, Hlangwane, and Monte Christo—Relief of Kimberley

CHAPTER V

Passage of Tugela forced and Colenso occupied—Another move back across the river to Hlangwane and Monte Christo—The Boers at length routed and Ladysmith is relieved—Entry of Relief Force into Ladysmith—Withdrawal of H.M.S. *Terrible's* men to China—I spend a bad time in Field Hospital—General Buller's army moves forward to Elandslaagte—Boers face us on the Biggarsberg

CHAPTER VI

End of three weary months at Elandslaagte—A small Boer attack—The advance of General Buller by Helpmakaar on Dundee—We under General Hildyard advance up the Glencoe Valley—Retreat of the Boers to Laing's Nek—Occupation of Newcastle and Utrecht—We enter the Transvaal—Concentration of the army near Ingogo—Naval guns ascend Van Wyk, and Botha's Pass is forced—Forced march through Orange Colony—Victory at Almond's Nek—Boers evacuate Majuba and Laing's Nek—Lord Roberts enters Pretoria—We occupy Volksrust and Charlestown

CHAPTER VII

Majuba Hill in 1900—We march on Wakkerstroom and occupy Sandspruit—Withdrawal of H.M.S. *Forte's* men and Naval Volunteers from the front—Action under General Brocklehurst at Sandspruit—I go to hospital and Durban for a short time—Recover and proceed to the front again—Take command of my guns at Grass Kop—Kruger flies from Africa in a Dutch man-of-war—Many rumours of peace

CHAPTER VIII

Still holding Grass Kop with the Queen's—General Buller leaves for England—Final withdrawal of the Naval Brigade, and our arrival at Durban—Our reception there—I sail for England—Conclusion

CHAPTER IX

Gunnery Results: The 12-pounder Q.-F. Naval gun—Its mounting, sighting, and methods of firing—The Creusot 3″-gun and its improvements—Shrapnel fire and the poor results obtained by the Boers—Use of the Clinometer and Mekometer—How to emplace a Q.-F. gun, etc., etc.

APPENDIX I

Hints on Equipment and Clothing for Active Service

APPENDIX II

Extracts from some of the Despatches, Reports, and Telegrams regarding operations mentioned in this Journal

APPENDIX III

Diary of the Boer War up to October 25th, 1900

APPENDIX IV

The Navy and the War: A Résumé of Officers and Men mentioned in Despatches for the Operations in Natal

LIST OF ILLUSTRATIONS

- TWENTY THOUSAND MEN ENCAMPED UNDER GENERAL BULLER
- A BATTERY CROSSING THE LITTLE TUGELA
- NAVAL BATTERY OF 4.7's AND 12-POUNDERS AT DURBAN
- NAVAL BRIGADE PITCHING CAMP AT FRERE, DECEMBER, 1899
- NAVAL GUNS IN ACTION AT COLENSO
- LIEUT. BURNE'S GUNS FIRING AT SPION KOP
- 4.7 EMPLACED ON HLANGWANE
- COLT GUN AT HLANGWANE FIRING AT BOERS
- NAVAL 12-POUNDERS ADVANCING AFTER ALMOND'S NEK
- 4.7 ON A BAD BIT OF ROAD
- BRINGING IN A BOER PRISONER
- IN CAMP AT GRASS KOP
- ONE OF LIEUT. HALSEY'S NAVAL 12-POUNDERS
- LIEUT.-GENERAL SIR H. J. T. HILDYARD, K.C.B.
- CAPTAIN PERCY SCOTT, C.B., R.N.
- NAVAL 12-POUNDER EMPLACED
- BOER GUN POSITIONS AT COLENSO
- CAPTAIN E. P. JONES, R.N.
- MAP

With the Naval Brigade in Natal: 1899-1900

CHAPTER I

Outbreak of the war—The Transport Service and despatch of Army Corps from Southampton—Departure of a Naval Brigade from England and landing at Capetown and Durban—I join H.M.S. *Philomel*.

During a short leave of absence in Scotland, after my return from Flag-Lieutenant's service in India with Rear-Admiral Archibald L. Douglas, that very kind friend, now Lord of the Admiralty, appointed me (5th October, 1899) to the Transport Service at Southampton, in connection with the embarkation of the various Army Corps for the war in South Africa. As the summons came by wire, I had to leave Stirling in a hurry, collect my various goods and chattels in London, and make the best of my way to Southampton. I reported myself at the Admiralty Transport Office on Monday the 9th, and at once commenced work, visiting certain ships with Captain Barnard, the Port Transport Officer, and picking up the "hang" of the thing, and what was wanted. Captain Graham-White, R.N., came down in the afternoon to take charge of our proceedings. From that date up to the 22nd, or thereabouts, we Transport Lieutenants simply had charge of certain vessels fitting out, and had to inspect for the Admiralty the many freight and transport ships which came in from other centres, such as London, Liverpool, etc., to be officially passed at Southampton; among others the *Goorkha* and *Gascon*, two Union Liners, came particularly under me, and I shall always remember the courtesy of their officials, particularly Captain Wait and the indefatigable Mr. Langley, who saw that we transport officers were well looked after on board each day. Everything in connection with this Line seemed to me during my time at Southampton to be very well done, and so our work went swimmingly.

Besides myself were Lieutenants McDonald, Nelson, and Crawford, R.N., as Transport Officers, and we co-operated with a staff of military officers under Colonel Stacpole, D.A.A.G., with whom we got on very well, so that we ran the work through quickly and without a hitch. Sir Redvers Buller left Southampton in the *Dunottar Castle* on the 15th October, and we all saw him off; in fact, McDonald and I represented the Admiralty at the final inspection of the ship before sailing. There was, of course, a scene of great enthusiasm, and many people were there, among whom were Sir Michael Culme Seymour, Alexander Sinclair his Flag-Lieutenant, and Lady and Miss Fullerton. All this time we were more than busy inspecting and getting ships ready up to the 22nd, when the departure of the First Army Corps commenced; we got away five transports that day within half an hour of each other, all taking some 1,500 men; they were, if my memory serves me, the *Malta, Pavonia, Hawarden Castle, Roslin Castle,* and *Yorkshire*; the next few days we did similar work from 8 a.m. till dark, getting away about three ships a day on an average.

During the week Commander Heriz, R.N., and myself, representing the Admiralty, inspected the hospital ships *Spartan* and *Trojan* before their start; they had been fitted out under the Commander's superintendence, and were perfect; in fact, one almost wished to be a sick man to try them! All these continued departures aroused great public interest; on one day we had the Commander-in-Chief (Lord Wolseley), Lord Methuen, Sir William Gatacre, and many other Generals; and on another the Duke of Connaught came to see the 1st Bn. Scots Guards off in the *Nubia* and gave them a message from the Queen; he came again a few days later to see his old regiment, the Rifle Brigade, off in the *German*, and he and the Transport Officers were photographed many times. I was told afterwards that my own portrait appeared very often in the cinematographs of these scenes, which were then very popular and were exhibited to crowded audiences in all the London and Provincial Music Halls and elsewhere. I was very pleased on this occasion to meet my old First Lieutenant of the *Cambrian*, now Commander Mark Kerr, R.N., who was also seeing the Rifle Brigade off with a party of relatives whom I took over the *Kildonan Castle*.

Here I may mention, to show the different rates of speed, that the *German* carrying the Rifle Brigade, actually arrived at Capetown some hours after the *Briton* (in which I myself left later on for South Africa), although it started ten days before us. I have very pleasant recollections of being associated with Major Edwards of the Berkshire Regiment in embarking the Reserves of the 3rd Bn. Grenadier Guards in the *Goorkha*, which ship I had been superintending for so long; I was able to get their Commanding Officer, Major Kincaid, two good cabins, for which I think he was much obliged to me. These Reserves were going to Gibraltar to pick up the main Battalions of their regiment which took part later on (3rd and 4th November) in Lord Methuen's actions at Belmont and Graspan.

After the 27th October the transport ships left Southampton in ones and twos, and we were not so hard pushed; in fact, the work was becoming rather monotonous, till, on the evening of the 2nd November, our Secretary, Mr. Alton, R.N., rushed up to me with a wire telling me to be prepared immediately to leave for the Cape. I was very pleased, and thought myself extremely lucky to get out to the scene of war with a chance of going to the front; and after saying a hurried good-bye to all my friends I left Southampton on the 4th November in the *Briton*; my father[1] saw me off and gave me some letters of introduction; Lord Wolseley also kindly wrote about me to Sir Redvers Buller; all my old colleagues of the Transport Service gave me a most cordial send-off, and we steamed out of the docks about 7 p.m. in heavy rain, which did not, however, damp the enthusiasm of hundreds of people who waited to see the last of us. In saying farewell to the Transport Service I could not help thinking how much courtesy and assistance we transport officers received from the captains and officers of all the ships under our inspection, and how much we admired their keen feeling and hard work in the interests of the public service. I hope this may be recognised when war rewards are given.

Our voyage was a good one, being calm enough after the first day, and all going well up to Madeira (where I landed for the sixth time) as well as on the onward voyage in which we went through the usual routine of ship life until we arrived at the Cape on Monday, 20th November. The Bay was full of transports, and they seemed still to be pouring in every hour; we did not hear much news except that Ladysmith was still safe, and we at once entrained for Simon's Bay, a pretty train journey of about an hour and a half, where the fleet were lying. Now commenced the bad luck of the Brigade "wot never landed," we all got drafted to various ships instead of going to the front in a body as we had hoped and expected, and my lot was to join the flagship *Doris*. Much to our disappointment a Naval Brigade had been landed the day before our arrival for Lord Methuen's force; we ourselves were therefore regarded for the moment as hardly wanted, and the Admiral was, we were told, dead against landing any more sailors. So we were both afflicted and depressed. I had, however, a pleasant time on the *Doris*, and found myself senior watch keeper on board. At night many precautions were taken in the fleet; guards were landed in the dockyard with orders to fire on any suspicious boat, and a patrol boat steamed round the fleet all night up to daylight with similar orders; we ourselves often went on shore for route marching and company drill and had a grand time.

I may mention, in passing, that all the bluejackets who were landed at Simon's Bay for shore duty were fitted with khaki suits, viz., tunics and trousers and hat covers, drawn from the military stores. With the trousers the men wore brown gaiters, and each man was provided with two pairs of service boots; they all wore their white straw hats fitted with khaki covers and looked very workmanlike in heavy marching order. The Marines also wore khaki and helmets, and had stripes of marine colours (red, blue and yellow) on the helmets to distinguish the Corps. Each batch of bluejackets that were sent to the front, about twelve men in a batch, was allowed two canvas bags to hold spare clothes and other gear, and took three days' provisions and water. The haversacks were all stained khaki with Condy's fluid, and the guns were all painted khaki colour.

We saw a great many people at Capetown, and while there, Colonel Gatcliffe, Royal Marines, the head Press censor, told Morgan and myself a lot of instructive facts about the work at the Telegraph Offices, and how all foreign telegrams in cipher to South Africa giving news to the Boers, as well as those from them, had been stopped. Some 300 telegrams sent after Elandslaagte by Boer agents at Capetown had been thus suppressed. When we saw Colonel Gatcliffe he was busily engaged passing telegrams, which had to be read and signed by him at the Telegraph Office before they were allowed to be despatched.

All went well at Simon's Bay until November 24th, when we heard of Lord Methuen's fight and heavy casualties at Belmont, followed soon by news of the heavy loss (105 killed and wounded) incurred by the Naval Brigade at Graspan chiefly among the marines. I think that the general idea in the fleet was admiration for our comrades and gratitude to Lord Methuen for giving the Navy a chance of distinction; but I am told these views were not shared by our Chief. A force of forty seamen and fifty marines were now ordered off to the front at once to fill up these casualties. Naturally we all wanted to go, but the Admiral could not send us and drafted us off to various ships, my own destination being H.M.S. *Philomel*, then at Durban, which I reached in the transport *Idaho*, a Wilson Liner. We had on board a Field Battery and other details with six guns and 250 horses. I was much interested in the horses, who had a fine deck to themselves and were very fit; they were in fact *'Bus* horses, and very good ones.

There were some Highland officers and others on board who had been wounded and were now going back to Natal after recovery; they told us how cunning the Boers were in selecting positions; one saw nothing of them, they said, on a hill but the muzzle of their rifles; they are only killed in retreat; they pick out any dark object as a man, such as a great-coat, training their rifles on it so as to fire directly he rises and advances. One of the officers told us how he saw at Elandslaagte a Scotchman who had been put by the Boers in their firing line with his hands tied behind his back because he had refused to fight for them; apparently the man escaped uninjured and was taken prisoner with the rest after the fight by our Lancers, swearing when liberated many oaths of vengeance on the Boers. Colonel Sheil told one of our officers, Commander Dundas, who was in charge of him and other prisoners on board the *Penelope* at Simon's Bay, that the only fault of our men was their rashness, and our Cavalry did not, he said, throw out sufficient scouting parties, missing himself and others on one occasion by not doing so; the Boers had not reckoned, he said, on Naval guns being landed, and placed great reliance on European interference. In his opinion, the war would be over the moment we entered Boer territory, and everything seemed at the moment to point to this conclusion. These Boer prisoners, who were all got at Elandslaagte, talked English well, and appeared, by all accounts, to have a good feeling and respect for the English, but they were very down upon the capitalists and others whom they blamed for the war.

To-day, at sea, as I write this (28th November), a S.E. breeze makes it delightfully cool. Indeed, I found the climate of Capetown, although the hot weather was beginning, delightful; a regular champagne air and a very hot sun, yet altogether a nice dry heat which quickly brought all the skin off my face at Simon's Bay after one day's march with the Battalion up the hills. I expect to find Natal much damper, and no doubt it will be very wet and cold at night in the hill country.

Thursday, 30th November.—The wind which has been blowing in our teeth has now moderated, so we may reach Durban earlier than we hoped, as we are only about 300 miles off. I watched the battery horses being exercised and fed this morning; they are mostly well accustomed to the ship's motion, but it is amusing sometimes to see about a dozen stalwart gunners shoving the horses behind to get them back to their stalls and eventually conquering after much energy and language, and after desperate resistance on the part of the horses; these old 'Bus horses are strong and fit, and have very good decks forward and aft for their half-hour exercise each day; while they are exercising, their stalls are cleaned out and scrubbed with chloride of lime. It is most interesting to watch their eagerness to go to their food, for they are always hungry!

With the Naval Brigade in Natal: 1899-1900

A BATTERY CROSSING THE LITTLE TUGELA.

NAVAL BATTERY OF 4.7'S AND 12-POUNDERS AT DURBAN.

With the Naval Brigade in Natal: 1899-1900

Friday, 1st December.—We arrived at Durban at 5 a.m. and anchored in the roadstead. In the Bay are H.M.S. *Terrible* and *Forte*; also a Dutch man-of-war, the *Friesland*, a fine looking cruiser; there are also eleven transports at anchor. Inside the Bay are the *Philomel* (my ship) and *Tartar*, besides a lot of other transports, including my old friend the *Briton*. Durban is a striking place from the sea; very green and cultivated, and with rows of houses extending along a high ridge overlooking the town. It all looks very pretty and one might fancy one's self in England. A strong breeze is blowing, so it is quite cool. An officer from the *Forte* tells us that Estcourt is relieved and that the Boers are massing south of Colenso ready for a big fight. Our army have apparently to bridge some ravines before advancing. The guns of the *Forte* and *Philomel* are at Estcourt with landing parties. Commander Dundas and Lieutenants Buckle and Dooner join the *Forte* and I join the *Philomel*. Tugs came out at 1 p.m. and took us in over the bar; we passed close to the *Philomel* and were heartily cheered; then we went alongside the jetty, where staff officers came on board with orders. Commander Holland (Indian Marine) is here in charge of Naval transport and is an old acquaintance, as we met last year at Bombay. I got on board the *Philomel* without delay and found myself Captain of her, as her Captain (Bearcroft) had gone to take the Flag-Captain's place with Lord Methuen's force, and Halsey, the First Lieutenant, was at Estcourt with some 12-pounder guns. About thirty men of the *Philomel* are on shore under two officers, and one of her 4.7 guns is up at Ladysmith. I hear that all guns north of Pietermaritzburg are under command of Captain Jones, R.N., of the *Forte*; and, in fact, all the ships here at present, viz., the *Terrible, Forte, Philomel,* and *Tartar*, have landing parties at the front.

I reported myself to Commander F. Morgan, senior officer of the *Tartar*, who was pleased to see me as he is an old friend, I having served with him in 1894 in the Royal yacht (*Victoria and Albert*), from which we were both promoted on the same day (28th August, 1894). I also called on the Commandant of Durban, Captain Percy Scott of the *Terrible*, at his headquarter office in the town. I found him busily engaged in making-up plans and photos of Durban, as well as his designs for field and siege mountings for the 4.7 and 12-pounder guns, to forward to Admiral Douglas, my late Commander-in-Chief; he showed them to me, and ordered me to take over command of the *Philomel* for the present. I have met a lot of old friends, and find the ship itself clean, smart, and comfortable. The weather is changeable and very hot. Captain Scott has ordered martial law in the town, and everyone found in the streets after 11 p.m. is locked up. The story goes that Captain Scott himself was locked up one night by mistake!

Tuesday, 5th December.—Captain Scott sent on board a kind letter from the Governor of Natal (Sir Walter Hely-Hutchinson) who has spoken to Sir Redvers Buller about me. An early advance is expected on Colenso, and it seems on the cards that some strategic move will soon be made to outflank the Boers and commence relief operations on behalf of poor Ladysmith.

With the Naval Brigade in Natal: 1899-1900

CHAPTER II

I depart for the front with a Q.-F. Battery from H.M.S. *Terrible*—Concentration of General Buller's army at Frere and Chieveley—Preliminary bombardment of the Boer lines at Colenso—The attack and defeat at Colenso—Christmas Day in camp.

On the 6th December there was much rejoicing in the fleet on account of an order from Headquarters that a battery of eight Naval guns was to go to the front to reinforce Sir Redvers Buller. Lieutenant Ogilvy, of the *Terrible*, was appointed to command, while Melville of the *Forte*, Deas of the *Philomel*, and myself, were the next fortunate three who were to accompany it. The battery, drilled and previously prepared by Captain Scott and Lieutenant Drummond, entrained the next day (7th) for its destination; but as I had to remain behind awaiting a wire from Headquarters, I was unable to start till the next morning, when I left for Frere, accompanied by my servant, Gilbert of the Marines. What a day of excitement we passed through, and how much we, who were off to the front, felt for those left behind! I gave over command of the *Philomel* to Lieutenant Hughes, the men gave me three cheers, and I left Durban amid many farewells and congratulations at my good luck.

Reaching Pietermaritzburg early on the 8th, we went onwards after breakfast to Estcourt. The railway is a succession of sharp curves and steep gradients and is a single line only. All the bridges on the line are carefully guarded, as far as Mooi River, by Natal Volunteers. I was much struck with the outlook all the way to Estcourt; a very fine country, beautifully green, with a succession of hills, valleys, and small isolated woods; in fact, if the country was more cultivated one might have thought it England, but it seems to be mostly grass land and mealy (Indian corn) fields. At Mooi River a farmer got into the train who had been driven from his farm near Estcourt when the Boers invaded Natal; he had lost all his cattle and clothes, while everything on his farm had been wantonly destroyed, and the poor fellow was now returning to the wreck with his small daughter.

On reaching Estcourt in the afternoon we found to our dismay that we could not get on any further for the moment; so I walked up to see Halsey of the *Philomel*, at his camp about half a mile from the station, and took him some newspapers. We had a bathe in the Tugela River, and I afterwards met Wyndham of the 60th Rifles who was A.D.C. to the Governor of Ceylon while I was Flag-Lieutenant to Admiral Douglas, and we were mutually pleased to meet again so unexpectedly. The Somersets marched in during the course of the morning from Nottingham Road; they all looked very fit, but seem to have the somewhat unpopular duty of holding the lines of communication.

Here I met also Lady Sykes and Miss Kennedy, doing nursing; they were staying at a Red Cross sort of convent close to the station. Lady Sykes gave me some books and wished me the best of luck, at which I was pleased. I believe she is writing a book of her experiences in the war and I shall be much interested to read it when I get home. It came on to pour with rain, with vivid lightning, about 8 p.m., so I was thankful to be under cover at the station; the poor soldiers outside were being washed out of their tents, and some unfortunate Natal Mounted Volunteers, who only arrived an hour beforehand, had no tents at all and had a very poor time of it.

Eventually I got off by train next morning (9th) for Frere, Captain Reeves, R.S.O., of the Buffs, who did me many kindnesses later on, having secured a compartment for me in a carriage which was shunted for the night, and in which I was very comfortable, although disturbed by continuous shuntings of various trains and carriages which made one realize how much work was falling on the railway officials and employés. In our train were fifty Natal Naval Volunteers under Lieutenants Anderton and Chiazzari. I was much struck with their good appearance and their silent work in stowing their gear in the train, and I realized their worth all the more when they joined up later on with our Brigade; all staid, oldish men, full of go and well dressed, while their officers were very capable, with a complete knowledge of the country.

We reached Frere Station on the morning of the 10th, passing the sad sight of the Frere railway bridge completely wrecked by the Boers. I walked out to the camp and had never seen such a fine sight before; rows and rows of tents stretching for miles, and an army of about 20,000 men. I found our electric search-light party at the station waiting to go on, and I was thankful to get a breakfast with them. Eventually our train moved on to the camp of the Naval batteries, about 2-½ miles due north of Frere, and I at once marched up with the Natal Naval Volunteers, reported myself to Captain Jones, and joined my guns, finding all the rest of the Naval officers here, viz.: Captain Jones, Commander Limpus, and Lieutenants Ogilvy, Melville, Richards, Deas, Hunt, and Wilde, with half a dozen "Mids" of the *Terrible*. In camp were two 4.7 guns on the new field mounting, one battery of eight 12-pounders, and another of four 12-pounder quick-firers.

On Sunday afternoon (10th December) an impressive Church service was held in the open, with ourselves forming the right face of the square along with Hart's Irish Brigade. In the course of next day (11th) I rode up to see James' battery on the kopje to our front defending the camp, and got my first glimpse of Colenso and the country around, some ten miles off. I found that James's guns had very mobile limbers which he had built at Maritzburg, very different to our cumbersome wagons with guns tied up astern. In the afternoon Melville and I had tea with General Hart who was very agreeable and kind, and said he knew my father, and my aunt, Lady Brind, very well.

In the evening orders suddenly came for Limpus' battery of 4.7's, my two 12-pounders, and Richards' four 12-pounders to advance the next morning (12th) at 4 a.m. to Chieveley, some seven miles from the Boer lines; and here again I was in luck's way as being one of the fortunates ordered to the front. All was now bustle and hurry to get away, and eventually the line of Naval guns, some two miles long with ammunition and baggage wagons, moved out in the gray of morning over the hills, with an escort of Irish Fusiliers, who looked very smart, "wearin' of the green" in their helmets.

Photo by Middlebrook, Durban.

NAVAL BRIGADE PITCHING CAMP AT FRERE, DEC. 1899.

We reached Chieveley at 8 p.m. (12th), after a long, dusty march, and got into position next morning on a small kopje about two miles to its front, called afterwards "Gun Hill." Guns were unlimbered and shell pits dug, while the wagons were all placed under cover; we received orders on arrival for immediate action, and at 9.30 a.m. we commenced shelling the enemy at a range of 9,500 yards. The 4.7 guns on the right fired the first shot, my two 12-pounders followed quickly, and a desultory shell fire went on for some hours. At my position we dug pits for the gun trails in order to get a greater elevation, and we plumped one or two shots on the trenches near the Colenso Bridge. The shooting of the 4.7's, with their telescopic sights and easy ranging, was beautiful; shell after shell, many of them lyddite, burst in the Boer trenches, and we soon saw streams of Boer wagons trekking up the valley beyond, while at the same time one of the Boer camps, 10,000 yards off, was completely demolished.

All this time our Biograph friends from home were gaily taking views of us, and they took two of myself and my guns while firing. Of course, the anxious officers of batteries had to lay the guns personally at this early stage, and every shot was a difficult matter, as at the extreme range we were firing, with the lengthening pieces on, the sighting was rather guesswork, and we had to judge mainly by the explosion at a distance of five and a half miles. We were all done up after our exertions under a broiling sun, and hence were not used any more that day (12th). Behind us we saw miles of troops and transport on the march onwards, which gave us the idea, and also probably the Boers, that Buller was planning a forward attack; and indeed, late at night on the 13th, the 4.7 Battery was told to move on to a kopje two miles in advance; my own guns, with the Irish Fusiliers being left to protect the ground on which we were then camped.

Orders came shortly afterwards for a general advance to the Tugela, and Captain Jones told me that I had been given the rear and left to defend from all flank attacks, and that I was to move on at daybreak of the 15th to an advanced kopje and place myself under Colonel Reeves of the Irish Fusiliers. All was now excitement; the first great fight was at length to come off and our fellows were full of confidence.

At 2 a.m., pitch dark, after a lot of hard work to get our guns ready, we struck camp; up rode Colonel Reeves with his regiment and threw out an advanced guard, and out we tramped and crossed the railway. Here we found all the field guns and Infantry on the move, and had great difficulty in getting on; but at last, at 5 a.m., we reached the desired kopje where I had been sent on to select gun positions. Before us stretched the battlefield for four miles to Colenso and the river; the Boers across the Tugela occupied an enormously strong position flanked by hills, all their trenches were absolutely hidden, and gun positions seemed to be everywhere. The iron bridge of Colenso was plainly visible through my telescope and was intact, and to all intents and purposes there was not a soul anywhere in sight to oppose our advance.

The Naval Battery of 4.7 and the 12-pounders under Captain Jones quickly got into position in front of us, and on all sides we saw our troops being thrown forward in extended order, forming a front of about four miles, with Cavalry thrown out on the flanks and field batteries galloping up the valley to get into range at 4,000 yards. All was dead silence till about 5.30 a.m., when the Naval guns commenced a heavy shell fire on the Boer positions. It was a fine sight; shell after shell poured in for an hour on the Boer trenches at a range of 5,000 yards, and all was soon one mass of smoke and flame. Not a sound came in reply till our troops reached the river bank, when the most terrific rifle fire I have ever heard of, or thought of, in my life, was opened from the Boer rifle pits and trenches on the river bank which had completely entrapped our men. Colonel Long, in command of the Artillery on the right of the line, unwittingly or by order, led his batteries in close intervals to within easy rifle range of those pits, when suddenly came this hail of bullets, which in a few minutes completely wrecked two field batteries (the 14th and 66th Batteries), killed their horses and a large number of the men, and threw four of the Naval 12-pounders under Ogilvy into confusion, although he was fortunately able to bring the guns safely out of action in a most gallant manner, with the loss of a few men wounded and thirty-seven oxen.

Many brave deeds were done here. Schofield, Congreve, Roberts, Reed, and others of the R.A. specially distinguished themselves by galloping-in fresh teams or using the only horses left in the two batteries, and bringing two guns out of action. With others at this spot poor Roberts met a heroic death and Colonel Long was badly wounded.

The firing all along the river bank was now frightful; shells from well-concealed Boer batteries played continuously upon our troops; the sun was also fearfully hot without a breath of air; and about 9 a.m. we noticed a sort of retiring movement on the left and centre of our position, and saw men straggling away to the rear by ones and twos completely done up, and many of them wounded. A field battery on the left had a hot time of it just at this moment and drew out of action for a breather quite close to our guns. I myself saw a dozen shells from the Boers go clean through their ranks, although, happily, they did not burst and did but little injury. Our troops were admirably steady throughout this hot shell fire.

Our Naval guns on Gun Hill, at about 5,000 yards range, were hard at it all this time trying to silence the Boer guns, and the lyddite shells appeared to do great damage; but the enemy never really got their range in return, and many of their shells pitched just in front of my own guns with a whiz and a dust which did us no harm. A little 1-pounder Maxim annoyed us greatly with its cross fire, like a buzzing wasp; it was fired from some trees in Colenso village, and enfiladed our Infantry in the supporting line, which was in extended order; but it did not do much damage so far as I could see, although it was cleverly shifted about and seemed to be impossible to silence.

By 11 a.m. (15th) we saw that our left attack was a failure; exhausted men of the Connaughts and Borderers poured in saying that their regiments had been cut up; and, indeed, many of their officers and men were shot and many drowned, in gallant attempts to cross the Tugela. Soon the ground was a mass of ambulance wagons, and stretcher parties bringing in the wounded; and a mournful sight, indeed, it was! The centre attack also failed, our men retiring quite slowly and in good order.

On the right, where the object of the advance was to carry a hill called Hlangwane, which was afterwards recognised to be the key of the whole position, our men, owing to want of numbers, could make but a feeble attack and were unable, unsupported, to pass the rifle pits which had been dug all along the valley in front of the hill. The Cavalry were, of course, of no use behind a failing Infantry attack with a river in front of them, and although extended to either flank it never got a chance to strike.

At 1 p.m. all firing ceased, except an intermittent fusillade by the Boers on our ambulance tents till they saw the red cross, when this ceased; the troops were all retired in mass to their original positions, and I myself had to clear out my guns as best I could to our old camping ground in the rear. To crown all, it came on to rain heavily about 5 p.m. by which we all got a good wetting. On our march back I had a few minutes of interesting talk with General Barton.

For many days all sorts of rumours flew about as to our losses at Colenso, which we afterwards found to be ten guns captured, fifty officers and 852 rank and file killed and wounded, and twenty-one officers and 207 N.C.O.'s and men missing and prisoners, a sad and unexpected end to our day's operations. An armistice to bury the dead was asked for by our people, and agreed to, but I do not believe that the Boer losses were at all heavy; and I am persuaded that if instead of the insufficient heavy batteries at Colenso, we could have had at the front, say two more batteries of 4.7 guns and two batteries of six 6" Q.-F., the Colenso disaster might never have happened. Against the fire of such guns, for say a week, moved up properly to within effective range, with reconnaissances carefully made and with an Infantry attack well pushed home in the end, I do not think that the Boers could or would have stayed in their positions; and I am confirmed in this opinion by a good many after experiences.

Saturday, 16th December.—Had a peaceful night and slept well, all being very much exhausted by the previous day's fighting and hot sun; we were kept very busy marking out ground for the Naval batteries which were all massed once more on our old camping ground.

Sunday, 17th December.—Commenced shelling Colenso Bridge at noon with a view to destroy it; but after a few rounds the order was cancelled and we again returned to camp.

Monday, 18th December.—Stood to arms at 4 a.m., then went to general quarters for action, when the 4.7 guns opened fire at daylight on Colenso Bridge for about two hours with lyddite, at a range of 7,300 yards. Lieutenant Hunt, on the left, struck one of the piers with a shell and took the roof off a small house close by; otherwise not much harm was done. It was a frightfully hot and depressing day with a wind like air from a furnace; and, bad luck to it, directly the sun was down at 5 p.m. a heavy dust storm came on which covered everything in a moment with black filthy dust, followed by vivid lightning and drenching rain which was quite a treat to us dried-up beings. I myself succeeded in catching a tubful of water which ensured me a good wash and a refreshing sleep for the night.

With the Naval Brigade in Natal: 1899-1900

Tuesday, 19th December.—A cool nice morning and all the men in good spirits. At 8 a.m. the 4.7 guns opened fire again on Colenso Bridge. Lieutenant England's gun—the right 4.7 gun—knocked the bridge away; a very lucky and good shot, at which, needless to say, Sir F. Clery was very pleased.

Wednesday, 20th December.—Again a nice and cool day. In the evening I fired my 12-pounders at trees and villages to the left of Fort Wylie; the 4.7 gun, manned by the Natal Naval Volunteers, also did good work. We are now living like fighting-cocks, as the field canteen is open, with many delicacies, about half-a-mile to our rear. We also received unexpectedly to-day, with acclamation, lots of letters and English papers.

Thursday, 21st December.—Stood to arms at 4 a.m. and commenced firing about 6 a.m., in a very good light; my own guns were directed on the rifle pits 8,500 to 9,000 yards away, on the other side of the Tugela River. At this range the ammunition carries badly and the guns shoot indifferently. I put some common shells, however, into the enemy's rifle pits, but we are all getting tired of this sort of desultory firing and existence.

Saturday, 23d December.—About 8.30 a.m. the Commander-in-Chief and Sir F. Clery and Staff, accompanied by the foreign attachés, rode up to our guns and stayed for an hour sketching the hills on the right of Colenso, which I presume is now our objective. Mr. Escombe, late Premier of Natal, was also up with us all day watching our firing. Captain Jones also came to ask me to represent the Naval Brigade on the Sports Committee for Christmas Day; so I went down to General Barton's tent, met Colonel Bethune, Captain Nicholson, and others, and we arranged a good programme between us.

Sunday, 24th December.—No firing to-day. Church Parade at 8 a.m., when we brigaded with the Irish Brigade. A very large stock of beer, cakes, pine-apples, and other good things arrived in camp for the Natal Naval Volunteers; they gave a good share to our fellows who were very pleased, having none, and all are now busy preparing their plum-puddings for Christmas Day.

Christmas Day, 25th December. — We stood to arms at 4 a.m., but orders came for the guns not to fire. I was up at 5.30 a.m. to take my Sports party down to camp for the Brigade events. Our men won the Brigade Tug-of-war right out, and got great fun out of the wrestling on horseback on huge Artillery steeds, so that we came back to camp very elated. At 3 p.m. we marched down again for the finals in Sports; our fellows rigged up an Oom Paul and a Naval gent on a gun limber; this we dragged all round the camps and created quite a *furore*. The heat and dust were awful in the sports, but we pulled them off on the whole successfully, and all came back to camp tired out. I had my Christmas dinner with the Irish Fusiliers, who had drawn out an amusing menu of *Whisky Powerful, Champagne Terrible, Cutlets à l'Oom Paul,* and so on. I thought much of my people and friends at home, and was glad enough to get to bed without the prospect of any night alarm or attack, after such a big dinner.

With the Naval Brigade in Natal: 1899-1900

CHAPTER III

Life in Camp and Bombardment of the Boer lines at Colenso—General Buller moves his army, and by a flank march seizes "Bridle Drift" over the Tugela—The heavy Naval and Royal Artillery guns are placed in position—Sir Charles Warren crosses the Tugela with the 5th Division, and commences his flank attack.

Tuesday, 26th December.—We stood to arms at 4 a.m., and shelled the Boer camp and trenches for two hours during the day. The Biograph people, who are still with us, took a scene of the Tug-of-war, our Oom Paul, and then a tableau of the hanging of Kruger! Captain Jones came to give the Sports prizes away, which greatly pleased our men; he told me afterwards that he had selected my two 12-pounders and the 4.7 guns to advance with him when ordered, at which needless to say I was very much gratified. Another heavy dust storm, followed by thunder and heavy rain. On the few following days we went through our usual cannonading, following a new practice of firing at night by laying our guns just at dusk, placing marks to run the wheels on, and using clinometers for elevation at the proper moment. All our shells burst, and, we were told afterwards, with effect, greatly disturbing sleeping Boers in Kaffir kraals at Colenso.

Friday, 29th December.—Again more firing at a new work that the Boers were making, apparently for guns. Seeing an officer on a white horse directing them, we banged at them all and cleared them off. Again a heavy storm, but sunshine reached us during it in the shape of boots and great-coats from Frere, for which we were all grateful. The following day was wet and cold. I went to camp to try and buy poor young Roberts' pony, but the price was too high for me. Lord Dundonald came to arrange with Captain Jones a sham night attack on the Boer lines which happily did not come off as it was a horrible wet night.

With the Naval Brigade in Natal: 1899-1900

Photo by Middlebrook, Durban.

NAVAL GUNS IN ACTION AT COLENSO.

New Year's Day, 1900.—At midnight of the old year my middy, Whyte, and myself turned out, struck sixteen bells quietly on a 4.7 brass case, and had a fine bowl of punch, with slices of pine-apple in it, which we shared with our men on watch, wishing them all a happy New Year. Good old 1899! Well, it is past and gone, but it brought me many blessings, and perhaps more to come. We gave the Boers some 4.7 liver pills, which we hope did them good. All our men are well and cheery, but our Commander has a touch of fever, so that I am left in executive charge of the men and camp. Winston Churchill came up to look at our firing. During the next few days, in addition to our firing, our 12-pounder crews started to make mantlets for the armoured train; a very big job indeed, as they had to cover the whole of the engine and tender, afterwards called "Hairy Mary," as well as the several trucks. The officer in command congratulated our men on their work under the indefatigable Baldwin, chief gunner's mate of the *Terrible*, who was in charge. The military also started entrenchments and gun pits on the hill, which we call "Liars Kopje"; at dusk they came to a standstill over some big boulders that the General asked us to remove, which was a compliment to the powers of the Navy. We soon made short work of the boulders, much to the General's satisfaction, and got on fast with the mantlets. Still heavy rain at night.

With the Naval Brigade in Natal: 1899-1900

Thursday, 4th January.—Again more firing. My own 12-pounder crews and those of Richards' guns hard at the mantlets for the armoured train, and doing the job very well. On the 2nd, Lord Dundonald rode up and arranged an attack on a red house 6,000 yards from us and supposed to contain some of the enemy, but we found nobody at home. We were all glad to receive letters from home to-day. I was busy all day shifting one of my 12-pounder gun wheels for a new and stronger pair of skeleton iron ones, just sent from Durban, in view of a feint to the front with the object of drawing the Boers away from Ladysmith.

Saturday, 6th January.—This feint was made and we had no casualties. Poor Ladysmith! Our men there are hard pressed and must have a bad time; very heavy firing all day, and we heard by heliograph that the Boers had made a heavy attack in three places, although, happily, repulsed with heavy loss (including Lord Ava) to ourselves. We have Bennet Burleigh, Winston Churchill, Hubert of *The Times*, and many others, constantly on Gun Hill looking at our firing.

Sunday, 7th January.—From Sir George White's signals we realize what a close shave they had yesterday in Ladysmith. A nice cool day and no firing; in fact, a day of rest. We attended Church Parade at 6 p.m. with the 2nd and 6th Brigades. The Boers are as usual in the trenches working hard, while our time just now is spent in rain and constant calls to arms.

Wednesday, 10th January.—A move at last, and I received orders to join General Hildyard's Brigade with my two guns, while the others were attached to other Columns. We were all hard at work to-day loading up wagons, and I was busy copying a large map of the country which our Commander lent me. In the evening General Hildyard sent for me on business, and I sat down with him and his Staff to dinner, including Prince Christian, Captain Gogarty (Brigade Major), and Lieutenant Blair, A.D.C. General Hildyard was very kind, and said he was glad I was to go with him; and the next morning I moved off my guns at daylight, and arrived at the rendezvous by the hour named. It was a fine morning, although the wet and soft ground gave me doubts about getting our guns across country. But off we started; the Cavalry scouting ahead, then the East Surreys, Queen's, and Devons, and the 7th Battery Field Artillery, followed by my guns escorted by the West Yorks. About a mile from Chieveley we had to cross a drift in which my wagons went in mud up to the tops of the wheels, and one gun got upset, which I got right again with the assistance of three teams of oxen and a party of the West Yorks. It was indeed a job, because the ground was like a marsh, and our ammunition wagons, with three tons' weight on them, were half the time sunk up to the axles; but we all smiled and looked pleased while everybody helped, and in six hours we were clear and on the road. We were all done up with the shouting and hot sun, and the General ordered us a two hours' rest while he took the Brigade on to Pretorius' farm, which we ourselves reached at 6 p.m., crossing another bad drift on the way. The men were absolutely done up, and we were glad to arrive and find ourselves in a fine grassy camp with plenty of water. General Hildyard called me up and said he was pleased with the splendid work we had put through that day. On our left were miles of baggage wagons of various Brigades going into camp along a road further west of us.

Thursday, 11th January.—Shifted my ammunition to fifty rounds per gun to lighten the wagons, and moved off at 5 a.m., passing General Hildyard who was looking on at the foot of the camp. We marched with the whole force to Dorn Kop Nek and then halted; the General and others, including myself, riding up to a high kopje to examine the Boer position on the Tugela at about 8,800 yards off. Prince Christian Victor came and sat on a rock by me and had a good look at the position through my telescope which he borrowed. The General ordered one of my guns up this kopje, and we brought it up with a team of oxen and fifty men on drag ropes to steady her. It was an awful climb, and the ground was strewn with boulders; the poor gun upset once, but we got it up at last into position on a beautiful grass plateau on top with a clear view of the Boer positions. The Queen's Regiment, who were our escort this morning, carried fifty rounds of ammunition up the kopje for me, and I shall always remember how on all occasions we received the greatest assistance from the Queen's and West Yorks. The General pushed on with the R.A. and the rest of the troops and reconnoitred the enemy from the next kopje. Eventually we were all ordered back to camp, and I had a great job in getting my guns down the hill again. I think it was worse than going up.

Friday, 12th January.—Prince Christian (Acting Brigade Major) and I had a short talk together; we touched on a scheme of mine for making light limbers for our guns. In the afternoon I rode out to General Clery's camp, three miles to the west, to see our Naval guns, but found they had been pushed on with Lord Dundonald's Cavalry to hold ground leading to Potgieter's Drift. I dined with Captain Reed of the 7th Battery, R.A., who knew my R.A. brother well in the 87th Battery. I found I had met him last year at the Grand National, and it is quite curious that I meet out here everyone that I ever knew.

Saturday, 13th January.—Sent Whyte, my middy, a nice fellow and useful to me, over to Frere on a horse to see about many things I wanted for the battery, and at 9.30 a.m. read out to my men on parade General Buller's address to the troops, dated 12th January, 1900. This is the text of it. "The Field Force is now advancing to the relief of Ladysmith where, surrounded by superior forces, our comrades have gallantly defended themselves for the last ten weeks. The General commanding knows that everyone in the force will feel as he does; we must be successful. We shall be stoutly opposed by a clever unscrupulous enemy; let no man allow himself to be deceived by them. If a white flag is displayed it means nothing, unless the force who display it halt, throw down their arms, and throw up their hands. If they get a chance the enemy will try and mislead us by false words of command and false bugle calls; everyone must guard against being deceived by such conduct. Above all, if any are even surprised by a sudden volley at close quarters, let there be no hesitation; do not turn from it but rush at it. That is the road to victory and safety. A retreat is fatal. The one thing the enemy cannot stand is our being at close quarters with them. We are fighting for the health and safety of comrades; we are fighting in defence of the flag against an enemy who has forced war on us from the worst and lowest motives, by treachery, conspiracy, and deceit. Let us bear ourselves as the cause deserves."

Sunday, 14th January.—Church Parade at 6 a.m. with the West Yorks, Devons, East Surreys, and Queen's. About 8 a.m. a wagon and team crawled up to our camp; this turned out to be the light trolley I had sent for and which Lieutenant Melville had kindly hurried forward from Frere. I was awfully pleased to see it as our load before was absurdly heavy. The General was also quite glad to see and hear of the new trolley. At 2 p.m. in came my new horse from Frere, and a bag of excellent saddlery; the horse was in an awful state; he had apparently bolted on getting out of the train at Frere and injured two Kaffirs who tried to stop him; then the Cavalry chased him and caught him ten miles from Frere towards the Drakensberg mountains. The poor animal was very much done up and I found him afterwards a fine willing beast.

Monday, 15th January.—Struck tents and limbered up ready to march at 6 a.m., and moved off in rear of the 7th Battery R.A.; they have been very good to us all along, shoeing ponies and giving us water. A nice cool morning, and all in good spirits. We soon passed the first drift across a spruit about four feet deep; my guns just grazed the top of the water but luckily we had taken care to stuff up the muzzles with straw. The bullocks had a very hard pull, more especially as my men were obliged to ride across the gun wagons. The General looked on and we got on very well; all working, laughing, joking, and helping, especially our good friends the Tommies. We marched across a green veldt, with the usual kopjes at intervals; and after about eight miles passed through the camp of the Somersets who came out to see us go by and were very cordial; about a mile further on we crossed the Little Tugela Bridge, and had a very heavy pull shortly afterwards across our last drift, which was a bad one. Countless bullock wagons, mule carts, and transport of all descriptions of the Clery, Hart, and Coke Brigades extended for miles along the two roads leading to our advanced position. We were delighted to see a river at last, and men and horses had a fine drink. After a meal in pelting rain I rode on to report to General

Hildyard, and had tea with him and his staff, including Prince Christian; they are all always very nice to me.

Tuesday, 16th January.—A stream of transport wagons is still crossing the drift this morning, and the Drakensberg mountains look very grand and beautiful in this clear air. We drew fresh meat to-day in our provisions. What a surprise and a treat! The Boer position on the Big Tugela lies six miles off; and here Dundonald and his Cavalry, with one 4.7 gun, are watching the enemy who are working day and night at their trenches. About noon, Colonel Hamilton, of General Clery's Staff, rode into our camp and told me that orders had come for my guns to proceed at once into position with Lieutenant Ogilvy's battery. He asked me how long I should be. I said two hours to collect oxen and pack up, and so we were ordered to march at 1.45 p.m. I was very sorry to be suddenly shifted again out of General Hildyard's Brigade, and I asked him to intervene if we were again detached, which he promised to do. We marched up to time, and got to camp about 5 p.m., escorted by a troop of the Royal Dragoons. As usual, it came on to pour; everything was quickly a sea of mud, and the men in their black great-coats, marching along with the horses and guns mixed up with them, reminded one strongly of scenes in pictures of Napoleon's wars. We found that we had to move on in an hour's time with Ogilvy's guns to a plateau further on. I rode out to see Captain Jones and the 4.7's in position, a grand one on top of a very steep cliff kopje some 1,000 feet above the Tugela; the plateau selected for our 12-pounder guns was some 600 feet lower down and 2,000 yards nearer the enemy. We had a tough march out, and did not get to our plateau till 11.30 p.m. I had a snack and gave the others all I could, and the great Maconochie ration and beer will never be forgotten, that night at any rate. I myself turned in to sleep under a trolley, just as I was, and very tired we all were after our hard day.

Wednesday, 17th January.—Out at daybreak to bring our 12-pounders into action. The drift over the Tugela, about half-a-mile to our right front, had been seized by Dundonald, and a howitzer battery had been pushed across some 2,000 yards nearer than ourselves, supported by the King's Royal Rifles, the Scottish Rifles, the

Durhams, and the Borderers; to our right front was also to be seen the Engineer balloon, under Captain Phillips, R.E., being filled with gas. About 10 a.m. a message came up from General Lyttelton to bring four guns into action on our left flank, which I did at once under Ogilvy's orders, and a little later Captain Jones rode down to us and told us to support Sir Charles Warren's advance to our left across the river. I opened fire with my right gun, and got the range in two shots, after which the whole four guns opened fire and burst several shells over the correct spot. I heard that Sir Charles Warren signalled in the evening to say we had by our fire put two Boer guns out of action and made them retire, and we were all delighted. His force was plainly to be seen occupying the ridge about 6,000 yards to our left front. The firing of the howitzer battery was very fine to-day; also our 4.7 guns did well. The howitzers landed salvos of their shells, six at a time, all bursting within fifty yards of one another and right on the Boer works on the sky-line, where our Naval 4.7's were also working away at a greater distance off. As no tents were allowed us I again slept in my clothes under a wagon.

Thursday, 18th January.—A beautiful morning, and we were all up at daybreak commencing a slow firing at the Boer trenches, and many fine shots were made; the howitzers, during the afternoon, pushed on about 500 yards nearer the enemy under cover of three small kopjes. Looking at the position from our plateau one wondered how the Boers could have allowed us to get here and cross the river unopposed. If we had been resisted we must have had an awful job, both here and at the Little Tugela. All our army experts are surprised, and we think we must have caught them on the hop, as they don't reply to our artillery fire. Still, they are opposing Sir Charles Warren's advance as well as they can, and very hard fighting is going on to our left, although we only hear the shots and see the flashes of our guns, with volleys of musketry, while the enemy are hidden behind a high hill called Spion Kop. The panorama before us is magnificent; and the Tugela, our bugbear at Colenso, lies before us, beautiful, meandering, and apparently conquered. At 5 p.m. a demonstration in force against the trenches at Brakfontein was ordered, and we commenced rapid firing with eight guns, making very fine practice and sending off some 600 shells to cover our

Infantry advance which was pushed on right up to the foot of the Boer kopjes and about 1,500 yards from their trenches. The Engineer balloon floated proudly in the air watching the operations. We retired at dusk, the object being to draw the Boers to their trenches and to relieve Sir Charles Warren's left attack which was advancing very slowly. We laid our guns at dusk and fired them every half-hour during the night.

Friday, 19th January.—We began firing again at daybreak, General Lyttelton and Staff looking on. They told us that our guns had shot very well the evening before. A very hot day. The fighting on the left seems to be heavier and more distant, and all sorts of rumours are current as to demonstrations and successes.

Saturday, 20th January.—Firing as usual. We hear again heavy firing on the left. About 3 p.m. our balloon went right out over the Boer trenches, while our Infantry attacked in force on the right and demonstrated in front in extended order; we kept up our firing, while James's guns which had been pushed across the river took the right hills, and with the howitzers put a Boer Pom-pom out of action. The balloon did well; it was fired at by the Boers with Maxims and rifles, and was hit in several places; in fact, Captain Phillips, in charge of it, had his forehead grazed by a bullet. During the afternoon my right gun trail smashed up and I had to employ all the talent near at hand to repair it. With a baulk of timber from the Royal Engineers we finished it, and at the same time shifted the wheels to a beautiful pair of gaudily-painted iron ones from Durban. I now call it the "Circus Gun."

Sunday, 21st January.—A very hot day. The armourers and carpenters still hard at work on my gun trail. Orders came for two guns to advance across the river, and Ogilvy told me off for that honour. By dint of hard work my right gun was finished by 11 a.m., and I inspanned and went off two hours afterwards. A very steep hill was the only thing to conquer going down, and we successfully crossed the Tugela in a Boer punt—guns, oxen, and my horse. We got the guns up to our new position by 6 p.m., and found ourselves about 4,200 yards from the enemy's trenches, with James's guns on our right. We had a cordial meeting with the Scottish Rifles; they had been a week in their clothes, with no tents or baggage, so I put up one of our tarpaulins for their mess tent and we enjoyed a real good dinner. At 9 p.m. up came Ogilvy to our position, to my surprise, as he had received sudden orders to bring the rest of the guns on across the river; the road and river must have been very nasty in the dark, but Ogilvy is a clever and capable fellow, who is always determined, sees no difficulties, and invents none.

CHAPTER IV

Spion Kop and Vaal Krantz—General Buller withdraws the troops and moves once more on Colenso—We hold Springfield Bridge—Buller's successful attack on Hussar Hill, Hlangwane, and Monte Christo—Relief of Kimberley.

Monday, 22nd January.—We placed the battery of six guns at daybreak in a kloof between two kopjes, in a half-moon formation, commanding the old position near Spion Kop, at about 4,500 yards, mine being in the centre. I was in charge all day and fired shots at intervals. The wind was too high for balloon reconnoitring. My first shot, a shrapnel, at the left part of Spion Kop, disabled twenty of the enemy digging in the trenches, so we were afterwards told by native scouts; and we were praised by those looking on for our accurate firing. We had now our telescopic sights on the guns, and very good ones on the whole they were, although we found the cross wires too thick and therefore hid an object such as a trench which at long range looks no more than a line. I found my deflection by a spirit-level on the trail, to test the inclination of the wheels one way or the other. There was very heavy fighting to-day on our left. Sir Charles Warren is in fact forcing his way on, and we hear reports of 400 of our fellows being killed and wounded, and the Boer trenches being taken by bayonet charges. So far as we know, General Buller's object is to outflank the Boers on the left, and then when Sir Charles Warren has done this, to attack in front and cut them off.

Tuesday, 23rd January.—Another day, alas, red with the blood of our poor fellows. Sir Charles Warren continued his operations at 1 p.m., and from then till midnight the fight raged. Musketry and guns booming all round, the Maxims and Vickers 1-pounder guns, being specially noticeable. At daylight we ourselves stood to guns and concentrated our fire on the Boer trenches and positions to the front and right, in order to draw the enemy away from Warren's force; while the Infantry with us (Rifle Brigade, King's Royal Rifles, Durhams and Scottish Rifles) made a demonstration in force to within 2,000 yards of the main trenches under cover of our fire. The attack under Warren got closer and closer each hour, and we could watch our fellows, apparently the Lancashire Brigade, storming the top of Spion Kop, in which, I afterwards heard, my father's old regiment (the Lancashire Fusiliers) bore a splendid part. Meanwhile our own attack on the Brakfontein trenches was withdrawn, and we brought our guns into action on the left to assist the operations on Spion Kop but soon had to desist for fear of hitting our own men. The fight raged all day and was apparently going well for us. At 4 p.m. came a message from General Buller ordering the King's Royal Rifles and Scottish Rifles to storm Spion Kop from our side, which they did, starting from our guns and making a prodigious climb right gallantly in a blazing heat and suffering a considerable loss. Poor Major Strong, with whom I had just breakfasted, was one of the wounded and, to my great sorrow, died of his wound. Our guns meanwhile were searching all the valleys and positions along the eastern slopes of Spion Kop; but it was all unavailing, as we were apparently forced to retire after heavy losses during the night. We ourselves were all dead beat, but had to be up all night with searchlights working on the Boer main position; but what of poor Warren's force after five days' constant marching and fighting!

LIEUT. BURNE'S GUNS FIRING AT SPION KOP.

4.7 EMPLACED ON HLANGWANE.

Wednesday, 24th January.—No more firing and many rumours; but at last it was a great surprise and blow to us to hear a confirmation of the report that Warren's right had been forced to abandon Spion Kop during the night, and to be also told that we ourselves were to go back to our old plateau in the rear. I had my guns dragged up to Criticism Kop with great labour by eighty of the Durhams, who are now our escort; and with the Rifle Brigade we hold the three advanced hills here, while Ogilvy has been moved back across the river. We hear of a loss of some 1,600 men, the poor 2nd Bn. of the Lancashire Fusiliers specially suffering heavily;[2] there is therefore great depression among all here, a cessation of fire being ordered, and nothing in front of us except ambulances. Our mail came in during the evening and I was very pleased to get letters from Admiral and Mrs. Douglas. We feared a night attack, so had everything ready for the fray. I was on the watch all night with Whyte, but our search-light kept off the danger and all remained quiet.

With the Naval Brigade in Natal: 1899-1900

Thursday, 25th January.—A quiet day, the Boers and our own ambulance parties burying the dead on Spion Kop. And so went the next few days, we shelling the Boers at intervals although sparingly. Rumour says that General Buller is confident of beating the Boers in one more try, and is shortly going to try it. May the key fit the lock this time! He seems determined, and we all hope he will be at last successful.

Monday, 29th January.—We are firing as usual. Colonel Northcote of the Rifle Brigade came over from his kopje to see me, and I proposed the construction of two rifle-proof gun pits on the river bank, to which he agreed. A very hot day and raining heavily at night.

Wednesday, 31st January.—We have orders to watch carefully the right of the Boer position. I let Mr. Whyte fire a dozen shells, which he did very well, and I finished my gun pits, and very good ones they are. Just at dark up came an officer from General Buller with an order that we were to retire our Naval guns at daybreak to the plateau, which we had to do much to our disappointment, moving off at daybreak next morning and taking the guns in a punt across the river. I learnt to my great sorrow that poor Vertue of the Buffs, my friend of Ceylon days when he was an A.D.C. to the General there, was killed at Spion Kop, and I am much depressed as I liked and admired him immensely.

Friday, 2nd February.—The Boers are busy burying their dead on Spion Kop under a flag of truce, so we have a quiet day and no firing.

Saturday, 3rd February.—The troops are all again on the move; no less than nine field batteries are pushed over the river with some Battalions of Infantry, while Boers are on the sky-line at all points watching us.

Sunday, 4th February.—Sir Charles Warren arrived on our gun plateau with his Staff, and pitched his camp close to my guns. I found that Sir Charles knew my father, and he told me that the Boers had had a severe knock at Spion Kop and were ready to run on seeing British bayonets; he spoke of his plans for the morrow and of our prospective share in them. My share is to be a good one, as I am to have an independent command and am so actually named in the general orders for battle. I went over the plan of battle carefully with Captain Jones, R.N., and our Commander, who thought Pontoon No. 3 was the weak spot.

Monday, 5th February. — A fateful day of battle. At daybreak we stood to our guns, but it was not till 6.30 a.m. that our Artillery, no less than seven batteries, advanced under cover of our fire. On the left were the 4.7 guns on Signal Hill; my two 12-pounders were on the gun plateau in the centre, and on the right, on Zwartz Kop, were six more of our 12-pounders under Ogilvy. The broad plan of attack was a feint on the left and then a determined right attack. This developed slowly; the Artillery and Infantry advanced, and we all shelled as hard as we could for some hours, when the Infantry laid down just outside effective rifle range from the Brakfontein trenches, and the Artillery, changing front to right, withdrew from the left, except one battery, to assist in the centre attack on Vaal Krantz. Our Naval guns went on shelling the left where the Boer guns were well under cover and were very cleverly worked. About 12 noon the Infantry withdrew from the left and it was evident that our feint had fully succeeded in its object, *i.e.*, to get the enemy drawn down to their trenches and stuck there. The Artillery, after crossing No. 2 Pontoon, were drawn up in the centre shelling Vaal Krantz, while Lyttelton's Brigade was pushed forward to attack it and succeeded in reaching the south end of it. Our own firing on the left was incessant. I found afterwards that I had fired 250 rounds during the day, and I had many messages as to its direction and effect from Sir Charles Warren, and General Talbot-Coke, who was just behind us with his Staff. Little firing during the night. Very tired.

Tuesday, 6th February. — At it again at daylight, the Boers commencing from their 100 lb. 6" Creusot at 6,000 yards to the east of Zwartz Kop. I had suddenly got orders during the night from Sir Charles Warren to move my guns off the plateau and join Buller's force at daybreak at the east foot of Zwartz Kop, so I moved off at the time named, feeling very thankful that I had my extra oxen to do it. We had some miles to go, over a vile road, and on the way we passed the 7th Battery R.A. and some Cavalry and ambulances. All this, meeting us on a narrow and badly ordered road, delayed us so much that it was 8 a.m. before I was able to report my guns to the Commander-in-Chief, which I did personally; he turned round and said, rather pleased, "Oh, the Naval guns are come up," and, pointing me out the Boer 6" Creusot and a 3" gun enfilading our Artillery, he asked me if I could silence them; the 6" was at 6,500 yards and the 3" at 10,000 yards, so I replied, "Yes, the 6"," and by the General's order I brought my guns into action about 200 yards away from him and his Staff. As I was preparing to fire my right gun, bang came a 100 lb. shell right at it, striking the ground some twenty yards in front and digging a hole in the ground of about six feet long, covering us with dust, although happily the shell did not burst but jumped right over our heads. This was followed by a shrapnel which burst, but the pieces also went right over our heads. After hard pit digging, I tried for the 3" at 9,000 yards, with full lengthening pieces, with my left gun, but I could not range it; so we kept up a hot fire with both guns on the Boer Creusot, which was also being done by the two 5" guns in front of us and by our Naval battery on the top of Zwartz Kop. We silenced this gun from 8.30 a.m. to 5 p.m. when it again opened on us (with its huge puff of black powder showing up finely), but without doing us much harm. At 11 a.m. the Boers brought some field guns up at a gallop to Vaal Krantz, running them into dongas or pits about 6,000 yards away from us, and then sending shrapnel into our troops on the Kop and trying to have a duel with us; we quickly silenced them, however, as well as a Pom-pom in a donga about 4,000 yards off, and they beat a retreat over the sky-line. I here found my telescopic sight very useful for observing every movement while personally laying guns. The General sent me many messages by his Staff, and was pleased at our driving off the guns. As the day passed, the cannonade became fast and furious and our attack advanced but slowly; we silenced most of the Boer guns by 5 p.m. and slept that night as we stood. I had the Boer 100 lb. 6" shell (which had fallen close to us without bursting) carried up the hill to show the Commander-in-Chief and Staff; they were all interested but rather shy of it, but one of them took a photo. We picked up many fragments of shells which had fallen close to us during the day and from which all of us had narrow escapes, for we were in a warm corner. General Hildyard and Staff who were sitting close by us at one part of the day had a 100 lb. shell fired over them which just missed Prince Christian.

Wednesday, 7th February.—Dawn found us still fighting on this the last day of our attempt to relieve Ladysmith from this side; heavy firing commenced at daybreak, and we did our best to keep down the Boer fire, the 4.7 Naval gun on Signal Hill making fine practice. Meantime our troops now on Vaal Krantz, viz., Hildyard's East Surreys, Devons, and West Yorks, pushed the attack or held their trenches under heavy fire, while we were trying to silence the enemy's guns. By this time the long range of hills to the east of Brakfontein was all ablaze from our shells, and also one flank of Vaal Kop. All looked lurid and desolate, and at times the cannonading was terrific, the Boer 6" with its black powder vomiting smoke and affording an excellent mark. At 4 p.m. the Engineer balloon went up in our rear to reconnoitre, and brought down a disheartening report of unmasked Boer guns and positions which would enfilade our advance from here all the way to Ladysmith; so that after a Council of War the Commander-in-Chief decided to retire the troops; my orders from Colonel Parsons, R.A., being to make preparations to withdraw my two guns to Spearman's Kop as soon as the moon rose, and to cover the retirement. In fact, according to his words the Council of War decided that while we could get through to Ladysmith from here, we should be hemmed in afterwards owing to the new positions disclosed by Phillips' balloon report. It was just dusk; Infantry and Artillery were being hastily moved up to cover the retirement, and after loading up our ammunition off we ourselves went. My poor men were very done up after the constant marching, firing, and working ammunition of the last three days; we had, in fact, shot off no less than 679 rounds, and the sun was awful the whole time. The withdrawal was very well carried out in the dark; we ourselves followed the ammunition column, and the Field Artillery followed us. As the foot of Gun Hill was completely blocked I brought my guns out down by the Tugela, ready to cover the troops; and we slept as we stood, while a constant stream of Artillery, Infantry, and ambulances were struggling to get up the steep hill; indeed, it was a most memorable day and night. Poor Colonel Fitzgerald of the Durhams was carried past me in a stretcher about 5 p.m. shot in the chest with a Mauser. I had known him before when holding the kopjes over the river with his regiment; he insisted on talking to me and sat up to have a cup of tea, and I was glad to hear afterwards that he had eventually recovered. Our total casualties for the three days were about 350; our Infantry had done brilliantly; and, while we were all savage at having to withdraw, we were confident that the Commander-in-Chief knew best, and indeed it seems from information received later on that he did the right thing.

Thursday, 8th February. — At daylight the Boer 6" went on shelling us at 10,000 yards but did little damage, so I got up the hill about 9 a.m. after a hasty breakfast, and passing Sir Charles Warren's tent got into my old position on the plateau, finding the 7th Battery R.A. holding the hill close alongside. My men were quite done up, so that the temporary rest was acceptable, although we had to keep a sharp look-out, and twice silenced Boer guns firing on our Infantry at 6,500 yards from Spion Kop. At noon the kopjes in front were evacuated, our pontoon taken up, and the Boer punt sunk by gunpowder. So good-bye to the Tugela once more; all our positions gone and the Boers down again at the river. At dusk I got permission to withdraw my guns over the ridge on account of sniping, and it was well I did so as the Boers came very close to us during the night.

Friday, 9th February. — Got orders from the Commander-in-Chief to withdraw with others on to Springfield Bridge; we were almost the last guns off, and had a hot march of eight miles escorted by a party of the Imperial Light Infantry under Captain Champneys. How we did enjoy a bathe from the river bank, as well as our sleep that night! It was all quite heavenly.

Saturday, 10th February. — About 9 a.m. I was ordered by Colonel Burn-Murdoch of the Royal Dragoons to bring my guns up to his entrenched camp behind the bridge to assist in its defence. I had breakfast with him and he seemed very nice. He is now Brigadier-General and Camp Commandant, and we are left in defence here, to protect Buller's left flank, with "A" Battery Horse Artillery, the 2nd Dragoons and 13th Hussars, the Imperial Light Infantry, and the York and Lancasters. The rest of the troops had all gone to Chieveley. The day was very hot again, and I was very glad to give the men another rest, with fresh butter, milk, chickens, and fruit to be had, brought in by Kaffirs from neighbouring farms. Just think of it!

Sunday, 11th February.—Again very hot. About 7 a.m. there was a heavy rifle fire to the N.E.; our Cavalry pickets were in fact attacked, and as I saw Boers on the sky-line, I got leave to open fire, but did no damage, as the hill, we afterwards found out, was some eight miles off. So much for African lights and shades, which, after eight months' experience of them, are most deceptive. It turned out that our Cavalry pickets had been surprised by the Boers unmounted in a donga, and unluckily Lieutenant Pilkington and seven men were taken prisoners, and several men wounded—a bad affair.

Monday, 12th February.—Another awfully hot day which made me feel feverish. We were busy in fortifying our gun positions, but otherwise I had a quiet day in the mess of the York and Lancasters, a very nice regiment. At 4 p.m., much to our joy, rain and thunder came on and cleared the heavy air. Glad to hear that a Naval 6" gun has been sent up to the front at last, and that Lord Roberts had entered the Orange Free State with a large force.

Tuesday, 13th February.—Still very hot, although again a welcome thunderstorm in the afternoon. Busy with fortifying and with taking more gun ranges with a mekometer borrowed from the York and Lancasters.

Wednesday, 14th February.—The Boers appeared in considerable force on the sky-line to the left of Portjes Kopje about 8 a.m. I was summoned with others by Colonel Burn-Murdoch to a Council of War, and afterwards rode out with him and Staff to reconnoitre the enemy and to look at country for gun work. We pushed up to a farm about 1,600 yards from the enemy; we were fired on at that distance and all returned about 4 p.m., when it was decided to attack the

Boers next day. They are some 9,000 yards off the camp, and seem to have no guns. During our reconnoitring we saw a hare on the Kop, the first game I have come across as yet in South Africa.

Thursday, 15th February.—At 6 a.m. the Horse Artillery and Cavalry were pushed out to attack, and my guns advanced to a kopje at 8,000 yards. But to our annoyance the Boers had made off during the night and we had nothing to do. We received an English mail to-day, much to our delight, and it brought a sketch in the *Daily Graphic* of my father inspecting a detachment of the St. John's Ambulance Brigade. My servant Gilbert in hospital with fever, poor fellow.

Friday, 16th February.—A red-letter day, and all quiet in camp. Fitted rollers under my gun trails. News came that General French had relieved Kimberley, and there was much cheering in camp.

Sunday, 18th February.—We heard heavy firing all day, which turned out to be General Buller attacking Hlangwane and Monte Christo Hills, to the right of the Boer position at Colenso, but on our side of the river. The positions were brilliantly taken at the point of the bayonet; and all in camp are very cheerful at hearing of Cronje being in full retreat, Magersfontein evacuated, and Methuen free to move. This must be the beginning of the end. Raining hard, for the rains of February are on us at last.

Tuesday, 20th February.—Still heavy rain and tropical heat. Our trenches full of water. Heavy firing on Colenso side and good news of Buller's advance.

CHAPTER V

Passage of Tugela forced and Colenso occupied—Another move back across the river to Hlangwane and Monte Christo—The Boers at length routed and Ladysmith is relieved—Entry of Relief Force into Ladysmith—Withdrawal of H.M.S. *Terrible's* men to China—I spend a bad time in Field Hospital—General Buller's army moves forward to Elandslaagte—Boers face us on the Biggarsberg.

Thursday, 22nd February.—General Buller occupied Colenso, and wired to our Commandant to join him with his whole force. The Cavalry left at 5 a.m. and at 2 p.m. the rest of us moved off, my guns being escorted by the York and Lancasters, with the Imperial Light Infantry in rear, the whole under Colonel Fitzpatrick. We made a quick march to beyond Pretorius' farm where we camped for the night.

Friday, 23rd February.—Off at daylight in a beautiful cool morning. On the west of the hill, where we rested to water and feed the oxen, Colenso was plainly visible, and we found heavy shelling going on. We reached Chieveley at 10 a.m. and going up to our old friend, Gun Hill, we joined Drummond with the 6″ Q.-F. gun, and pitched our camp. The 6″ gun looked a regular monster on its field carriage, and fired several times at Grobler's Hill, at 15,000 yards; I was struck by its smart crew of bluejackets and stokers, but the gun is much too far off the enemy. An English mail came in to-day.

Saturday, 24th February.—General Buller is shelling hard the kopjes at Pieters beyond Colenso, but our Infantry do not seem to be gaining an inch. As my guns were in reserve, I went up by train to Colenso, with Captain Patch, R.A. We were much interested, as we saw all the now famous spots where we had shelled the place out in December and January—the village and hotel being in ruins, and everything wantonly sacked and destroyed. I never saw such a scene in my life;

pianos pulled to pieces and furniture smashed up. I went on to the pont where Lieutenant Chiazzari was in charge, and met many wounded being carried across to the ambulance train; among others were General Wynne, and a poor officer of the Lancashire Brigade just dying with a bullet in his chest, also young Hodson of the *Terrible* ill with fever. We crossed the Tugela on planks over the ruins of the fallen railway bridge with a swirling torrent about a foot below us, as the river was now in flood. It was sad to see this magnificent bridge with all its spans blown up and fallen across the river, and one buttress demolished. Patch and I climbed up the kopjes beyond, saw the Boer system of trenches, and inspected the places where they had blasted the reverse slopes of the kopje, perpendicularly cut behind, and had got under safe cover from shell. The panorama of battle which spread out in front of us was most impressive with shells bursting close to us; our firing line was some two miles on, resting on small kopjes near Pieters that were taken during the night; our guns, great and small, were massed in or beyond Colenso behind small kopjes which gave a certain amount of cover; on the left were the 4.7 guns and four 12-pounders, then the 4.5 guns; and two miles to the right were other field batteries and Ogilvy's four 12-pounders across the river on Hlangwane, making some eighty guns in all. Behind the kopjes were massed our men in reserve, besides all the Horse Artillery and Cavalry and wagons. There was now very heavy Boer shelling over Colenso, giving our men a bad time of it; for instance the whole of our 5" crew of garrison gunners were killed and wounded by a shrapnel, and many of the 4.7 men were hit about the same time. Our own shelling was magnificent and deadly, all our fire being concentrated at one kopje about 6,000 yards off; the musketry fire was also very heavy all along the line. I never saw such a fine sight before. I returned from Colenso to my guns about 3 p.m., in an ambulance train, with Major Brazier Creagh. We are losing about 450 men a day and are advancing very slowly, while the Boers appear to be bringing up more guns on our left. No news from Ladysmith, but we were all glad to hear the brilliant news of the capture of Cronje and all his force by Lord Roberts, and the cheering in the fighting line on the news being communicated was wild. A very heavy musketry fire raged all night, and the Inniskillings in a night attack on Railway Hill lost a lot of men, in fact were cut up.

Sunday, 25th February.—Once more the Commander-in-Chief found his position untenable, and half of the guns were withdrawn in the night across to our side of the Tugela on to Hlangwane; all the wagons and stores were also shifted out of Colenso and the majority of the troops moved to the right to the Hlangwane and Monte Christo slopes. Colenso was still held in force however by the 10th Brigade under General Talbot Coke. Two of our 4.7 guns on platform mountings were now ordered up to Hlangwane from our hill, and were got into position with much labour at 2,500 yards by Lieutenant Anderton, Natal Naval Volunteers; they did very good work at that decisive range. There was to-day what we called a Boer Sunday, that is, a cessation of firing on both sides after a hard ten days of it; the day was wet and we were all washed out of our tents, some of which were blown clean down.

Monday, 26th February.—The attack still hangs fire while our troops are being massed on Hlangwane and Monte Christo. The shelling of Colenso by the Boers is still going on pretty heavily, and one only wonders how Naval 12-pounders like ours can be left here as they are, no less than six of our guns doing nothing at all. Drummond left the 6" gun under me for a time; and, on spotting a Boer gun on Grobler's Hill, I let drive at 15,000 yards, 28° elevation. As the shot only fell some 200 yards short, I recommended a move to closer range, but the gun eventually never was moved closer. While on Gun Hill we had several civilians from Pietermaritzburg and Durban looking on at the fighting. A very wet night, which made our positions a swamp, but I was warmed by a warning to be ready to move my own guns to the front.

Tuesday, 27th February.—A wire was handed to me in the night to join the 10th Brigade with the Yorks and Lancasters, and off we went at 6 a.m. in good spirits but in a thick drizzle of rain, passing along the eastern slope of Hlangwane and winding up a fearful road to the front. The Yorks and Lancasters at this point suddenly turned off, and feeling that something was going wrong I halted my guns and rode on to the Headquarters Staff, about half a mile on, finding the Infantry attack just about to commence, the men all looking very weary, and no wonder. I spoke to Ogilvy, who was there with his guns, and afterwards to General Buller, who was standing quite close surveying the general attack of our Infantry on the centre and right 3,000 yards ahead of us. The guns were giving the Boers lyddite and shrapnel, and the fighting line were cheering as kopje after kopje was taken. It was evident to my unpractised eye that we had the Boers on the run at last. I told the Commander-in-Chief that my guns had arrived, when he replied, "Why, you should be in Colenso," and turned to his Staff, saying that some mistake had been made. I therefore showed my written orders, and after reading them, the General said, "It is not your fault, but march to Colenso as quickly as possible"; and he detached Lord Tullibardine to show us the way; I had seen a good deal of him at Springfield. "The Pontoon bridge is up," he added; "you must use the Boer pont and so ferry across the Tugela." So off we went, and got to Colenso at 2 p.m. after a very hot march.

Photo by Middlebrook, Durban.

4.7 EMPLACED ON HLANGWANE.

The ground at the railway crossing which we had to cross was being heavily and accurately shelled, so leaving my gun train for a time in a spot safe from the bursting shrapnel I rode on to prepare the pont for our crossing the river. We got the first gun over to the Colenso side of the river after hard work, the rotten bank giving way and the gun being half submerged in the water; then the somewhat unhandy soldiers in charge of the pont capsized a team of gun oxen when half-way across the river by rocking the pont, and, nearly drowning the poor oxen, swam ashore themselves and left them to their fate. It was now 5 p.m. and as there were no men to do anything it was an impossible position, with the pont sunk in the middle of the flooded river; so that at dusk, after telling some soldiers who had come up from General Coke's Brigade in response to my request what to do to right the pont, I drew up my remaining gun and wagons on the south bank, and put the gun which was already across the river out of action under a guard below the river bank in case of any Boer swoop on it.

Wednesday, 28th February.—A red-letter day. Before daylight I set my men to work to bale out the pont and to get my second gun across the river with 100 rounds of ammunition, and also off-loaded and got over a spare wagon and 250 rounds more. All this was a terrible hard job; two empty military wagons trying to get across the drift at this spot were carried away before my eyes and only picked up a quarter of a mile down stream. At 11 a.m. I was able at last to march on to join General Coke's Brigade in Colenso, and to get my guns into position. I was very exhausted and was feeling rather ill, but I was able to dine with the General under a tarpaulin and had much talk over old times in the Mauritius in 1898. It was a very wet evening, and my men who were bivouacking with no tents had a bad time of it. The sudden cessation of firing most of the day seemed to foreshadow some change at the front, and we found afterwards to our joy that a detachment of the Imperial Light Horse under Lord Dundonald had ridden into Ladysmith at 6 p.m. unmolested by the Boers who were reported to be in full retreat.[3]

Thursday, 1st March.—Everything seems to feel dull and unprofitable; all the country round is deserted and Colenso is almost unbearable from the odour of dead horses. At about 11 a.m. the pickets reported Boers in force coming down Grobler's Kloof, but the party turned out to be our own men; some of the garrison Cavalry, in fact, riding in from Ladysmith, who told us that the Boers were in full retreat. In the afternoon I rode round Colenso. What a scene of desolation and dirt; huts and houses unroofed and everything smashed to pieces! Long lines of abandoned trenches, and the perpendicular shelters which the Boers had blasted out behind all the kopjes against shell fire plainly showed how well they knew how to protect themselves. The trenches, about a mile long, in the plain to the right of Colenso are very deep and are sandbagged; parts of them are full of straw; many shelters are erected in them; and holes are burrowed out and strewn with chips of cartridges and pieces of shell, bottles, and every imaginable article. Being somewhat curious as to the effect of our shelling which had gone on from the 10th December to the 12th January at this line of trenches, I rode along them and came to the conclusion that not one of our shells had actually hit these splendid defences, although no doubt our fire annoyed and delayed the workers in them. I picked up many curios here.

Friday, 2nd March.—Not a Boer to be seen within miles. Very hot and odoriferous here, and I feel queer and tired out although fortunately able to lie down all day. In the middle of the night had a sudden and alarming attack of colic and was in great agony. I really thought I was done for, but my men gave me hot tea and mustard and water which did me good.

Saturday, 3rd March.—Woke up feeling weak and ill, but as luckily there was no work on hand I was able to lay still under an ammunition wagon and was much revived with some champagne which my best bluejacket named House got for me from my friend Major Brazier Creagh of the Hospital train. The doctor from the Middlesex lines who came to see me in the evening told me he had been into Ladysmith and had found the garrison looking very feeble; the Cavalry were hardly able to crawl and could not therefore pursue the Boers; the rations had been reduced to one and a half biscuits per day per man in addition to sausages and soup called

Chevril, made from horseflesh. It seems that Ladysmith could have held out for another month, but the garrison had, after our failure at Spion Kop, given up all hope of our relieving them. Poor chaps! they have had an awful time of it. We learn that the Boers had left a huge unfinished dam of sandbags across the Klip River so as to flood out our shelter near the banks of the town; another week would have seen this really marvellous work completed; but luckily, as it was, our friends had to decamp in a hurry, leaving tents, wagons and ammunition strewn all over the neighbourhood; I wish I could add guns, but none were found, and I fear that the retreat took place for one reason only, viz., Kruger's fear of being cut off by Lord Roberts at Laing's Nek. Except for this I doubt whether we should ever have moved the Boers out of the Colenso position with our 30,000 men; indeed, I hear that the German Attaché said it was a wonder, and that his people would not have attempted it under ten times the number. As it is, we are all glad that General Buller has succeeded.

Tuesday, 6th March.—Nothing special to note except that wagons and ambulances have been pouring out of Ladysmith down Grobler's Hill during the last few days.

Wednesday, 7th March.—In the afternoon General Coke kindly came to wish me good-bye as his Brigade had received orders to sail for East London, and at the same time gave me orders to proceed to Ladysmith. Meanwhile the Naval Brigade under Lionel Halsey passed our camp on the way to Durban, and we drew up to cheer them and received their cheers in return. Poor fellows, they looked as weak as rats.

Thursday, 8th March.—We left Colenso at 5.30 a.m. with the 73rd Field Battery for Ladysmith. We were much interested on the Grobler's Hill road to see the Boer trenches and shelters, which were simply marvellous and made the place impregnable. The trenches were blasted out of solid rocks, some 6 feet, and some 6 to 8 feet thick, of solid rock and boulder; these were all sandbagged, fitted with shelters with burrowed-out holes, and were extended for a front of half a mile facing Colenso. On the other side of the road, slightly higher up, was another line of similar trenches, while the road itself was defended by a series of stone conning towers—to use a Naval term—all loopholed and commanding the entire passage. It was a wonderful revelation to us after the "prepare to dig trench" exercise prescribed by our own drill book. The Governor of Natal, Sir Walter Hely-Hutchinson, happened to ride by when our Naval guns were drawn up, and when he found that I was in command he sent for me, was very kind, and said he would write to my father to tell him he had seen me. Although still feeling ill from dysentery I tried not to make much of it, but I could no longer ride my horse so got on a wagon. We moved on to Ladysmith at 4 p.m. and were much interested in the various hills and positions *en route*; we passed over Cæsar's camp, which we found a very straggling uninteresting sort of place. The town itself lay on the left and was now used as a hospital; we passed along over the iron bridge where the troops from India were encamped, and much admired their khaki tents and green ambulances; and climbing the hill leading to the convent to join our Naval camp we found Ogilvy in command, who said, much to my regret, that the men of the *Terrible* who manned my own and their guns, were ordered to be withdrawn for service in China.

Friday, 9th March.—Having struggled long against my dysentery I am now compelled to go on the sick list; and feel it to be a great blow, after all my trouble and training, that my *Terrible* bluejackets are to go. Good fellows. It seems bad for the force, putting aside all personal reasons, that all our trained men now well up to the country we fight in, should thus suddenly have to go, and that Mountain Battery gunners and others should be sent to fill their place. The men, however, seem glad to go back to their ships after all their severe work; and indeed the bluejacket is in some respects an odd composition; he turns up trumps when there is work to be done, but he is not always content with existing conditions and likes changes! Sir Redvers Buller is very pleased with us, so says the Naval A.D.C., and the telegrams just read out to the Naval Brigade from home are extremely complimentary.

They are (1) from the Queen—"Pray express my deep appreciation to the Naval Brigade for the valuable service they have rendered with their guns"; (2) from Admiral Harris—"The Lords

Commissioners of the Admiralty desire me to express to the Naval and Marine officers and Bluejackets and Marines who have been engaged in the successful operations in Natal and Cape Colony, the sense of their great admiration for the splendid manner in which they have upheld the traditions of the service, and have added to its reputation for resourcefulness, courage and devotion"; (3) from the Vice-Admiral Commanding Channel Squadron—"Very hearty congratulations from officers and men to Naval Brigade." We were all pleased at these wires, and especially that, among others, Sir Harry Rawson had not forgotten us.

Saturday, 10th March.—Alas, at last I have to go to our Field Hospital much against my will, while to add to my sorrow all my good men of the *Terrible* are starting off to rejoin their ship. We were all glad today to hear of Ogilvy's promotion to Commander for distinguished service in the field. He thoroughly deserves it.

Tuesday, 13th March, to Thursday, 22nd.—A bad time, and I can hardly walk a few yards without being tired. While in hospital, about the 15th, a frightful hailstorm came on, the hailstones being as big as walnuts and even as golf balls; the horses in camp broke loose and stampeded, tents were blown down and flooded; several poor enteric patients died from the wetting, and we had a very bad time. Meanwhile important changes have gone on; Ladysmith has been emptied of Sir George White's troops; Sir Charles Warren and General Coke are gone to Maritzburg; the Naval Brigade is broken up, and our Naval guns are turned over, alas, to Artillery Mountain Batteries. Captains Scott and Lambton are made C.B.'s; the *Powerful* has left for England, and the *Terrible* leaves for China; our flag is hoisted at Bloemfontein, and the tone of the Foreign Press has altered; still more troops are pouring out from England, and we hear that 40,000 more men are to be landed before April, which is a very good precaution.

Friday, 23d March.—There are rumours that the Boers have evacuated the Biggarsberg hills, and at any rate all our troops are moving on to Elandslaagte. The Dublins celebrated St. Patrick's Day on the 17th with great *éclat*, and all the Irish soldiers throughout Natal wore the shamrock. They have behaved splendidly all through the operations and it is a pity that the Irish nation is not more like the Irish soldier.

Sunday, 25th March. — Out of hospital to-day, but so weak that I can hardly walk a yard, so I have to give in and go down country much against my will. General Kitchener of the West Yorks told me of a private house of the Suttons' at Howick, near Maritzburg, and strongly advised me to go there; so I left Ladysmith on the 27th and got a warm welcome from the Honourable Mr. and Mrs. Sutton and their family who were most kind; and on the best of foods I soon began to pick up. The house is a very pretty combined country and farm house facing the Howick Falls, 280 feet high, of the Umgeni River. While here news came of the disaster at Sanna's Post and the capture of 500 of the Irish Rifles at Reddesberg, so we are all disappointed and think the end of the war further off than we thought. My twenty-seventh birthday on the 1st April passed quietly in this peaceful spot, and after a pleasant stay I left on the 13th, my lucky day, fairly well, although still a stone under weight. I was very sorry to leave my more than kind friends and hope to meet them again some day.

Saturday, 14th April. — Reached Elandslaagte and rejoined the Naval Brigade at the foot of the historical kopje which the Gordons and Devons stormed in October last. The 4.7's are on top in sandbagged emplacements, and the 12-pounders are in other positions on the right. We are with General Clery, in General Hildyard's Brigade, and we hold the right while Sir Charles Warren holds the left, of our long line of defence. The Boers face us a long way off on kopjes north of us beyond a large plain.

Sunday, 15th April (Easter Day). — All quiet here. About lunch time Commander Dundas and Lieutenants Buckle and Johnson of the *Forte* arrived to pay us a visit, and they were all very interested in what I and others were able to show them.

Tuesday, 17th April. — I feel much stronger and better now. Orders having come for General Clery's Division to withdraw to Modder

Spruit, it did so at 6 p.m., leaving the Rifle Brigade and Scottish Rifles with us, all under General Coke.

Friday, 20th April.—Nothing moving in front. I have been given James's guns to command as he has slight fever, and I have had all the work and worry of dragging them up this kopje, making roads and gun emplacements which are now too elaborate for my liking. Generals Hildyard and Coke came to look at my gun positions and said they were both glad to see me again; they have always been considerate and perfect to work under. General Hildyard has now Sir Charles Warren's (the Fifth) Division. I am very glad to be under him, although sorry that Sir Charles Warren leaves us, which he does to administer the Free State. Some sensation in camp to-day at Lord Roberts' comments on Spion Kop; undoubtedly he is very sharp and mostly right; he is now our one great hope out here and seems to be afraid of no one.

Saturday, 21st April.—At daybreak we were hurried out by reports of Boers in force to the front, and we saw several hundreds on the kopjes at 8,000 to 10,000 yards. We are now in a position on the hill where Elandslaagte was fought. The graves of some of our own men are here. In the centre of the hill are those of the Boers, and the remains of hundreds of dead horses and cattle are still lying about. The collieries of Elandslaagte lie two miles to our left; and further again to the left are the 5" military guns and two 12-pounders in emplacements, while our own Naval 12-pounders and the 4.7's are on this hill. Our right flank for some reason seems to be left practically undefended. At 7 a.m. the Boers brought a 15-pounder Creusot down on this flank and threw several shells just over us at 4,800 yards; our 4.7's and one of my own 12-pounders replied with shrapnel and silenced it. The Boers appear to be in force in front, moving backwards and forwards through Wessels Nek, so we have kept up a desultory fire all day. At night they fired the grass in front of us for about four miles; we were up all night expecting a night attack, but none came; we were well prepared for it, as the hill was defended by some 300 men in all round the guns.

Sunday, 22nd April.—At daylight stood to our guns in a heavy mist but no Boers reported. Received a box of fresh food from one of my kind friends, Mrs. Moreton, daughter of Mrs. Sutton of Howick.

Monday, April 23rd to Friday 27th.—Boers reported to be returning on Newcastle. The long-expected presents from England for the Naval Brigade from our good friends Rev. A. Drew, Miss Weston, Lady Richards, and Mr. Tabor, have at last reached us from Durban, where they have been lying for upwards of four months. As we have only sixty bluejackets left up here we are overloaded. I took some tobacco, a beautiful pipe in case, some books, and a neck scarf. After all this kindness from friends at home what can we do for them in return? Poor James, and also my servant Gilbert, have gone to hospital with enteric. I am myself not much up to the mark but am thankful to have command of guns again, and so try to keep well.

Monday, 30th April.—No events of importance during the last few days. Weather a trifle cooler. I rode over to the hospital on Saturday to see Gilbert who is very bad, poor fellow, and will have to go home. I gave him clothes and books and tried to cheer him up a bit. On my return I found a fine large parcel of clothes from my own people at home. Took the Naval Brigade to Church yesterday and marched past General Hildyard afterwards.

Sunday, 6th May.—Nothing has been stirring during this past week, and we are getting rather weary of the quiet. We have news from home of the Queen's inspection at Windsor of the *Powerful* men and of a fierce debate in Parliament on the Spion Kop despatches. We had our own Church service to-day.

CHAPTER VI

End of three weary months at Elandslaagte—A small Boer attack—The Advance of General Buller by Helpmakaar on Dundee—We under General Hildyard advance up the Glencoe Valley—Retreat of the Boers to Laing's Nek—Occupation of Newcastle and Utrecht—We enter the Transvaal—Concentration of the army near Ingogo—Naval guns ascend Van Wyk, and Botha's Pass is forced—Forced march through Orange Colony—Victory at Almond's Nek—Boers evacuate Majuba and Laing's Nek—Lord Roberts enters Pretoria—We occupy Volksrust and Charlestown.

Monday, 7th May.—Still at Elandslaagte. Rumours of a possible attack made us stand to guns before daylight, and it was well we did so, as at 5.45 a.m. a party of Boers tried to rush the station and were repulsed with slight loss on both sides; they managed to clear off in the dim light. The attacking commando became afterwards known as the "Ice Cream Brigade," being largely composed of Italians and Scandinavians.

Thursday, 10th May.—Rumours of a move. Poor Captain Jones is laid up with jaundice, and indeed all in camp are a little off colour. Nice letters to-day from my father and Admiral Douglas. The Middlesex and Halsey's guns are shifted over to Krogman's farm. Self busy putting to rights some of our wagon wheels which had shrunk from the tyres owing to the great heat and drought.

Friday, 11th May.—A great move this morning. The Dorsets trekked at daylight to hold Indudo Mountain and Indumeni on our right. General Clery's Division marched with Dundonald's Cavalry up Waschbank Valley, and the 5" have been shifted to cover this advance. We were much amused to-day in reading the first edition of the *Ladysmith Lyre* (Liar), which perhaps I may be forgiven for quoting, with songs sung by the garrison:—A duet by Sir George

White and General Clery, "O that we two were maying"; by Buller's Relief Force, "Over the hills and far away"; by the Intelligence Officer, "I ain't a-going to tell"; by Captain Lambton, "Up I came with my little lot"; then a letter from Ladysmith to Paradise Alley, Whitechapel:

"Dear Maria,

"This 'ere seige is something orful. We sits and sits and sits and does nothing. Rations is short, taters is off, and butter is gone. We only gets Dubbin. These blooming shells are a fair snorter; they 'um something 'orrid. 'Opin' this finds you as it leaves me,

"Your affectionate,
"Martha."

Among other amusing items was, "Mrs. K. says her dear Oom is getting too English: he no longer turns into bed in his clothes and boots."

Sunday, 13th May.—We got our marching orders at last about 11 a.m., and I was just in the act of mounting my horse in good spirits to ride off and see my guns brought down over Elandslaagte Kop, when something startled him and he bolted over the rocks near the camp; having only one foot in the stirrup I overbalanced and came heavily on my head and left shoulder and was knocked silly for twenty minutes with a gash over my eye to the bone. I was carried to my tent and kindly stitched up by Dr. Campbell of the Imperial Light Infantry, and being much shaken I was obliged to hand over command of my guns to poor Steel who was only just recovering from jaundice and had to trek off at 3 p.m. to Sunday's River Drift. By keeping very quiet in the 4.7 camp in Hunt's tent I got over my fall better than I expected, and was able to move on, with a bandaged head and a sore body, with the 4.7 Battery when they marched at daybreak on the 17th to Waschbank Bridge which we reached at about 11 p.m. after a very hot and dusty march—all done up and cross, and self in addition bandaged up and feeling altogether unlovely after a slow and horribly dusty ride of eighteen miles. The position of affairs now seems to be this: General Buller with Clery's Division (the 2nd) and the Cavalry have occupied Beith and moved on Dundee from which the Boers fled on the 14th with 4,000 men and eighteen guns. Thus, Buller is in Dundee; Lyttelton's Division (the 4th) is still near Ladysmith under orders to advance; and we (the 5th) are to move to Glencoe with all speed up Glencoe Pass and along the railway line route.

Friday, 18th May. — At 7 a.m. we trekked under General Hildyard and had a very trying march with dust, dust, dust, sometimes a foot thick, till arriving half-way to Glencoe we outspanned oxen. We found all the railway bridges and the culverts of the line, some twenty-eight all told, blown up along our line of march. The Boer positions we passed on the road were extraordinarily strong, as usual; and one can well understand why they held on to this place and the Biggarsberg ranges on each side, a position ten times stronger than any Colenso. We reached Glencoe about 5 p.m., and marching through it bivouacked for the night a mile beyond the town on the level uplands. Here we received orders to advance with all speed to Newcastle, where the Commander-in-Chief is with the 2nd Division; so on we moved by moonlight in a cloud of dust and passed the night on an awful rocky place at Hatton's Spruit, trekking on in the morning towards Newcastle; but when five miles on our march we received orders to move back to Glencoe as the line had broken down and there were no supplies for us at Newcastle. All disappointed, but back we had to go! The weather is bitterly cold, and although we have our tents, we are, no doubt for good reasons, not allowed to pitch them.

Sunday, 20th May. — Took over my guns from Steel feeling rather low with a plastered cut on my face. General Hildyard has congratulated us all on the hard work and marching of the last few days. Both he and his Staff have always a kind word for everyone, and I was greatly pleased when they and Prince Christian, on seeing me with my faithful guns once more, told me how glad they were that I had got so well over my fall.

Tuesday, 22nd May.—Busy getting my wagon wheels and guns right after their trek over the bad road, and obliged to send them into Dundee to be cut and re-tyred. I rode with Steel and Hunt to Dundee which is five miles off; it is a small and miserable place with tin-roofed houses, bare dusty surroundings, and awful streets. We saw poor General Penn Symons' grave with the Union Jack flying over it, and other graves marked by faded wreaths and wooden crosses. We had a talk with the Chaplain who said that the Boers had passed through on Sunday in full flight with all their guns. We rode back from this desolate scene, amid the dust of ages and smell of dead animals, wondering how poor General Symons ever allowed the Boers to occupy Talana Hill which is only half a mile from the town and completely commands it; in fact, there should never have been a Talana, and our troops did splendidly to retake it.

Wednesday, 23rd May.—Sudden orders to move off at 2 p.m., so all is rush and hurry. I rode once more at the head of my guns, and all went well with us except that one of the poor oxen broke a hind leg in the trek chains down a steep bit of road and had to be left behind and shot. For four hours after this our long line of march was stuck in a drift, but at last, at 11 p.m., we got over it and at 1 a.m. bivouacked at Dannhauser.

Thursday, 24th May.—The Queen's birthday. God bless her. Up at daylight, very cold, and no tents. Poor Captain Jones still very sick with jaundice. Steel also, following my example, got a bad fall on the rocks from his horse and is in Field Hospital. At noon we all paraded in line with the Naval Brigade on the right; General Talbot Coke made a speech and we gave Her Majesty three cheers from our hearts and drank her health in the evening.

Friday, 25th May.—Orders came to get our guns in position to defend the camp, so off I had to go to do this on one flank and Halsey on the other; and we lay out all day ready for an attack, with the cattle grazing just in front of us. To our right about fifty miles off is Majuba Hill.

Saturday, 26th May.—We left Dannhauser at daybreak—oh, how cold—marched with the 10th Brigade, and trekked on to Ingagane, meeting on the road Lyttelton's Division (the 4th), which was hurrying to the front. We reached Ingagane at 5 p.m., and met General Buller and Staff just as we were going into camp for the night. The General looked well; and the sight of him, somehow, always cheers one up, as one feels something is going to be done at once.

Sunday, 27th May.—Up at daybreak and awfully cold. We marched off to Newcastle, the fine Lancashire Fusiliers, my father's old regiment, doing rearguard just behind our guns. Met Archie Shee of the 19th Hussars who recognised me from old *Britannia* days, where he and I were together. He told me that my cousin Ernest St. Quintin of the 19th had gone home with enteric after the Ladysmith siege. On getting to the top of the hills overlooking Newcastle we were much struck with the view and the prettiness of the town which the Boers had hardly wrecked at all—quite the best I have seen in Natal from a distance. We went gaily down the hill and over a footbridge into camp where we found all three Divisions together, barring a Brigade pushed on with some 5" and 12-pounders to Ingogo. We hear that Lord Roberts is across the Vaal, and that Hunter is pushing up through the Orange Free State parallel with us, while the enemy are holding Majuba, Laing's Nek and tunnel, and Pougwana Hill to the east of the Nek, with 10,000 men.

Monday, 28th May.—Moved off with the 5th Division under General Hildyard towards Utrecht. After an eight-mile march we crossed the bridge over Buffalo River and Drift unopposed by Boers, and entered the Transvaal at last. We were the first of the Natal force to do so, so I record it proudly. At 9 p.m.—a very cold night—orders came for an advance on Utrecht, my guns and some Infantry under Major Lousada being left to hold the bridge and drift here. I visited all the salient points of defence and outposts from Buffalo River to Wakkerstroom Road and carefully selected my gun positions, then brought the guns, each with an ammunition wagon, up the ridge, a steep pull up, and placed them one commanding the Utrecht Road and one Wakkerstroom Road—unluckily one mile apart, which could not be helped. I put my chief petty officer, Munro, in command of the left gun and took the right one myself, riding between the two to give general directions when necessary. At night as no Boers appeared we withdrew the guns and wagons behind the ridge.

Wednesday, 30th May.—Drew the guns out of laager at sunrise and again got into position and arranged details of defence with Major Lousada so far as my own work was concerned. All was quiet however to-day, and we saw no Boers nearer than Pougwana. And so it went on for the next few days, during which the Landrost of Utrecht, after twenty-four hours' armistice, delivered up the town to General Hildyard, saying that he had done the same in 1881 to a British force which had never occupied it after all. So history repeats itself.

Saturday, 2nd June.—Marched along the right bank of Buffalo River towards Ingogo, while Lyttelton's Brigade moved on our right on the other side of the river towards Laing's Nek. After a pleasant trek across the open veldt, and therefore no dust, we reached De Wet's farm near Ingogo in the evening and bivouacked; a grand day marching right under Majuba and Prospect and yet no sign of the enemy. Had a short talk with General Hildyard and Prince Christian on the march, as they rode by my battery, reminding the latter that I had first seen him when I was in the Royal yacht in 1894 and took his father and himself about in her steam launch at Cowes—a very different scene to this. The Prince said he knew all along he had seen me before somewhere.

Tuesday, 5th June.—Rode to Ingogo and saw the spot where the fight took place in 1881, the huge rocks from which our fellows were eventually cut up by Boer rifle fire, the monument set up to the 3rd Bn. Royal Rifles, and some graves higher up of which one was to a Captain of the R.E. Poor, unlucky, but gallant Sir George Colley; he went from Ingogo to Majuba and there met his untimely death. The view from here of Laing's Nek was glorious at sunset, Majuba frowning on one side with Mount Prospect and Pougwana on the other, and the bed of the Ingogo River below in a green and fertile valley. The Boer position is very strong although our heavy Artillery ought to be able to force it.

Wednesday, 6th June.—All on the move, as the armistice which General Buller was trying to arrange with Chris Botha is up, the latter replying: "Our heavy guns and Mausers are our own and will be moved at our convenience; the armistice is over." We hear that Lord Roberts is in Pretoria and that Kruger has fled; but how unsatisfactory that this does not end the war. In fact, marching to Pretoria was the feature and romance of the war, and now must commence anxious and weary guerilla tactics which may last a long time. About dark in came orders to the Naval guns to move on and occupy Van Wyk to-night: and off we went through large grass fires and along awful roads, getting to the foot of the hill at about 1 a.m. with no worse mishap than the upset of one of my guns twice on huge rocks hidden in the long grass.

Captain Jones ordered me to go on up the hill during the night, leaving the 4.7 guns at the bottom; so we commenced a weary climb up Van Wyk (6,000 feet) on a pitch-dark night lighted only by the lurid gleams of grass fires which the enemy had set going on the slopes of the mountain. With thirty-two oxen on each gun it was only just possible to ascend the lower slopes, and thus we made very slow progress. But as Colonel Sim R.E. kindly showed me a sort of track up, on we toiled for six hours, my men not having had a scrap of food or a rest since starting while the night was deadly cold and dark. In the gray dawn, just as we were attempting the last slope which was almost precipitous, the wheels of one of the guns gave out and there we had to leave it till daylight, pressing on with the sound one and getting it up to the top exactly at daylight (7th June) in accordance with our orders, taking the gun and limber up separately, with all my oxen and 100 men pulling. We found the position was held by the 10th Brigade, and very heavy sniping going on down the N.W. slopes—a regular crackle of musketry.

I soon got my gun along the crest into an emplacement prepared by the Royal Engineers, and opened fire at once at 7,000 yards at a Boer camp on the slopes of an opposite kop; but finding the camp practically deserted we did not waste much fire on it. My men were now half dead with fatigue and cold, so we all got a short rest in a freezing wind.

Sir Redvers Buller, quite blue with cold, rode up about 9 a.m. with his Colonial guide, and carefully surveyed the position through my long telescope. Prince Christian also came up later to talk over the Boer position and seemed in great spirits. After a good look round we could not see many signs of the enemy in front, and he was just going off to report this, but at that moment the spurs of the berg opposite to us became alive with them at 6,000 or 7,000 yards off; they came in a long line out of a dip and donga and advanced in skirmishing order with ambulances in rear and a wagon with what looked like a gun on it. I opened fire at once and put my first two shells at 6,000 yards right into some groups of horsemen; we saw them tumbling about, so after about a dozen shots from my gun off they went like greased lightning, seeming to sink into the earth and evidently quite taken aback to find we had a gun in such a position. In a few minutes not a sign of them was left, and the Commander-in-Chief riding up appeared much pleased and congratulated us on our straight shooting; he seemed very satisfied that we had got the guns up Van Wyk at all, and rode off leaving us quite rewarded with his appreciation, besides that of General Hildyard and his Staff who were with him.

Up to about noon we had nothing but long range sniping going on, but to make all sure the 4.7 guns were sent up the hill by an easier and more circuitous road than we had come, and took up position in emplacements close to us. We on our part were busy all day completing our ammunition up to 100 rounds a gun from the wagons which we had been obliged to leave in the night half-way down the hill. Horribly cold! I slept in the open under a limber.

Friday, 8th June.—An attack on Botha's Pass arranged for 10 a.m. The 10th Brigade and Naval guns are to hold Van Wyk and cover the advance, with a range of 8,000 yards from the pass itself, and about three miles of valley and road between to search with our fire; the 11th Brigade is to attack in the centre, advancing along the valley to the foot of the pass; the 2nd Brigade of the 2nd Division to attack on the right, in echelon, and clear the slopes and spurs of the berg on our right flank; we ourselves to form the left of the line.

Our first objective was a conical high kop, called Spitz Kop, about 3,000 yards on our right and this was occupied without resistance by the South African Light Horse; our guns searched all the valleys and dongas up to the pass with a furious fire for some two hours assisted by May's batteries below us. We could hear General Clery pounding Laing's Nek with the two 4.7 guns on Prospect Hill and four 5" guns on our right, although Majuba and Pougwana were shut out by Mount Inkwelo from our actual view; and we knew that General Lyttelton had been detached to operate to the N.E. of Wakkerstroom. The attack developed about noon and we saw below us our Infantry and field batteries spread out in the plain like ants while we still pointed our guns ahead of them on to the top of the berg and pass. Up to the foot of the berg our men met with no resistance, but at last a furious fire of rifles and Pom-poms broke out on our right centre from Boers concealed in dongas and trenches on the spurs. Our gallant 11th Brigade, with the pressure eased by our fire and by the advance of the 2nd Brigade, took the hills and pass in grand style, and with small loss comparatively to ourselves. About 4 p.m. the enemy, driven up to the sky-line, lit large grass fires and cleverly slipped off towards the N.E. under cover of the smoke. We saw and fusilladed the Pom-poms through this smoke at 10,000 yards with the 4.7's, and at 5 p.m. we had the whole ground in our possession. Our troops in the valley were pushed on all night, and we ourselves also received orders to descend Van Wyk and press on. A shocking night; very wet and bitterly cold, with a heavy Scotch mist settled over us. Down Van Wyk we came, although delayed by our escort of Dublin Fusiliers losing their way all night in the fog, but the Dorsets helped us instead. We had a tough job coming down the steep hill in the mist but I had some fifty men on each of my guns to drag back and steady them, and we eventually got down to the lower ground without accident, but very much worn out and only just before daylight.

Saturday, 9th June.—At 6 a.m. moved on for Botha's Pass Road at full speed, and skirting a crest of hills overlooking a deliciously cool river, we soon came to the valley where our attack was advanced, and eventually got up the pass at dusk, at the tail end of a huge column all racing to get up first. If the Boers had properly entrenched the place it would have been impregnable. We bivouacked in Orange River Colony at the top of the pass, all in good spirits at our success and at being in a new country.

Sunday, 10th June.—Off at daybreak through delightful hard roads and veldt as compared with mountainous Natal; we can now realize Lord Roberts' fine forced marches on seeing the difference between these and the Natal roads. Our bullocks slipped along at the rate of three miles an hour, and passing farms flying white flags and flat veldt country we bivouacked for the night on Gansvlei Spruit, finding the boundary here of the Transvaal (a bend of the Klip River) quite close to us.

NAVAL 12-POUNDERS ADVANCING AFTER ALMOND'S NEK.

4.7 ON A BAD BIT OF ROAD.

Monday, 11th June. — Off at 5 a.m., and got our Naval guns in position to attack, but found that the Boers had evacuated the ground in front of us. Up and on at a great rate over the grassy veldt, the guns now marching in four columns and keeping a broad front. At about 1 p.m. sudden firing in front and the familiar whirr of Boer shells made us come into action at 4,500 yards on Almond's Nek Pass, through which our road lay. The Boers were evidently in possession, judging by the warm greeting of Pom-poms and the Creusot 5", which played on us without much damage. The troops were now all halted, and formed up for attack which was to commence in an hour's time. The Commander-in-Chief (Buller) directed the operations, carried out at 2 p.m. by the Infantry advancing in long extended lines, the 10th Brigade in the centre, the 11th on the right, and the 2nd on the left, the field batteries and Naval guns covering the advance with lyddite. The 10th Brigade, which had 3,000 yards of plain to cross and a small kop to take, dislodged the Boers and their Pom-poms quietly and steadily under a heavy rifle and gun fire, the noise being terrific, as the hills and ravines were smothered by shrapnel and lyddite; in half-an-hour the Boers were on the run again and their fire was silenced, after treating us with Pom-pom and 45-lb. shrapnel, one piece of which narrowly escaped my left foot—a detail interesting to myself to recall. The attack of the Queen's, East Surreys, and Devons, on the left of the pass, and especially of the Dorsets on the conical hill, was most gallant and irresistible. Thus, about 5 p.m., at dusk we were in possession of the ridges 5,000 feet high on the left and right of the pass, which we thought a great achievement, while the Cavalry and Horse Artillery were pushed on to complete the Boer rout, but darkness coming on prevented this. General Buller and his Staff rode along our guns evidently very pleased, and indeed the force had won a brilliant little victory which cleared our way effectually and turned Laing's Nek besides. The Boers lost, as we thought, about 140 killed, of whom we buried a good many, while our casualties in killed and wounded were 137; but we afterwards learnt from an official Boer list found in Volksrust that their losses on this occasion reached 500, chiefly from our shrapnel fire. General Talbot Coke who directed the centre attack congratulated Captain Jones on the fine shooting of the Naval guns, as did also General Buller who said it had enabled them to take the position in front of us with such small loss. Again bitterly cold, and we bivouacked for the night on the battlefield.

Tuesday, 12th June.—On again an hour before dawn through Almond's Nek; a thick mist came down, but all being eventually reported clear ahead we marched on towards Volksrust and bivouacked.

Wednesday, 13th June.—All our men in high spirits; the 11th Brigade, with the Naval guns, moved on Volksrust, while the 10th Brigade and Royal Artillery guns marched to Charlestown, and we thus occupied the two towns simultaneously. Volksrust is a cold-looking, tin-roofed town; all houses and farms are showing the white flag, the men are gone, and the women are left behind weeping for their dead. We captured here a store of rifles and ammunition besides wagons and forage, not to mention Boer coffins left in their hurried flight.

Thursday and Friday, 14th and 15th June.—At Volksrust resting on our laurels, and all in good heart, although feeling this bitter mid-winter cold. General Hildyard sent for names to mention in his despatches, and I believe I am one. As commanding the *Tartar* guns I was also very pleased to be able to mention six of my men, and am full of admiration of the way in which my bluejackets have worked, shot, and stood the cold and marching. To sum up our recent operations, they are:—March from Elandslaagte to Glencoe, reoccupation of Newcastle; crossing of Buffalo Drift and occupation of Utrecht; ascent of Van Wyk at night with guns; turning and capture of Botha's Pass; march through Orange River Colony and Transvaal in pursuit of the Boers; taking of Almond's Nek and occupation of Volksrust and Charlestown, with the strong position of Laing's Nek turned and evacuated by the enemy who are in full flight. This is all very satisfactory, and we hear of congratulations from the Queen and others to General Buller. The Boers have, however, with their usual cleverness and ability, got away their guns by rail, but we hope to get them later. We are now busy refitting wagons and gear for a further advance. I hope the services of the bluejackets in these operations, which have been invaluable, will receive the recognition they deserve at the end of the campaign.

CHAPTER VII

Majuba Hill in 1900—We march on Wakkerstroom and occupy Sandspruit—Withdrawal of H.M.S. *Forte's* men and Naval Volunteers from the front—Action under General Brocklehurst at Sandspruit—I go to hospital and Durban for a short time—Recover and proceed to the front again—Take command of my guns at Grass Kop—Kruger flies from Africa in a Dutch man-of-war—Many rumours of peace.

Saturday, 16th June.—Starting about 10 a.m. I rode over to Laing's Nek with Captain Jones and Lieutenants Hunt and Steel, taking Charlestown on our way and getting up to the railway tunnel where Clery's Division is encamped. The Boer scoundrels have blown down both ends of the tunnel, blocking up the egress, and putting a dead horse at each end! We found also a deep boring they had made over the top of the nek through the slate with the object of reaching the roof of the tunnel and exploding it; but this having failed, from our friends not getting deep enough, the damage is insignificant and the rail will be cleared by the Engineers within a few days. We rode along the top of Laing's Nek and looked at the trench, some three to four miles long, which the Boers had made there; it completely defends the nek from every point of attack and gives the defender, by its zigzag direction, many points for enfilading any assaulting party. In fact, the work is marvellous; the Boers must have had 10,000 men employed on it, the trench being some five feet deep on stone and slate, with clever gun positions, stretching from Pougwana, to the east of the nek, to Amajuba on the west, as we saw plainly later on from Majuba and elsewhere. We rode up Majuba Hill as far as we could, finding it a great upstanding hill with a flat top overlooking the nek. On the way we passed many small trenches and sniping pits evidently made for enfilading fire. From the top of the grassy slope (when it became too steep for the horses to climb) we commenced the ascent of the actual hill on foot, climbing, one might say, in the footsteps of the Boers of 1881 when they made the wonderful attack on Colley and turned his men off the top. Right well can we now understand how they did it; it is almost too clear to be credible to us, and one cannot but regret the omission of the English force to hold the spurs of the mountain when occupying the top, seeing that any attacking party, safe from fire from the top of the hill on account of the projecting spurs, could get up untouched to within a few feet of the top of this northern face; this is what the Boers did while holding poor Sir George Colley's attention by long-range fire from the valley below. We saw what must have been the very paths up which the Boers crept, and when it came to the point where they had to emerge the slope was precipitous but short; here, so records tell us, by a heavy rifle-fire while lying flat on their stomachs, they drove our men off the sky-line, and once at the top the whole affair became a slaughter. Climbing this last steep bit as best we could, we reached the flat top quite blown and found it about 300 yards wide with the well-known, cup-shaped hollow, in the centre of which lie our poor fellows buried in a wire enclosure—sad to say twenty-two bluejackets among them, beside Gordons, King's Royal Rifles, and others. An insignificant stone heap marks the place where poor Colley was shot, and on one stone is put in black-lead "Here Colley fell." The sky-line which our men held had only a few small rocks behind which they tried to shelter themselves but no other defence at all in the shape of a wall or trench. All the east and south faces overlooking the nek have now (nineteen years later) been very heavily trenched by the Boers at great expense of labour; they were evidently expecting we should attack and perhaps turn them out of Majuba, although the slope of the hill on the south side is quite too precipitous for such an operation. I picked up some fern and plants near where Colley fell, as a memento. We took an hour and a half to get down again, meeting General Buller and his Staff walking up to inspect the hill, and I rode back ten miles to Volksrust blessed with a headache from the steep climb and strong air. The view from the top of Majuba, showing the Boer trenches on Laing's Nek, was wonderful; well might they think their position impregnable and well might we be satisfied to have marched through Botha's Pass and forced the enemy to evacuate such an impregnable place with so little loss to ourselves.

With the Naval Brigade in Natal: 1899-1900

Sunday, 17th June.—Left Volksrust early to march on Wakkerstroom, news having come in that General Lyttelton was somewhat pressed and was unable to get on. Our march was uneventful, as we only passed the usual farms with white flags and batches of Dutch women—as mischievous as they pretend to be friendly. Bivouacking for one night we got to Wakkerstroom—a march of twenty-eight miles—on the 18th, bivouacking outside the usual style of town, very cold and gray looking, one or two tall buildings, and situated in a treeless valley at the foot of some high hills. Very cold and wet.

Wednesday, 20th June.—Moved away from this spot the same way we came, and had no incident except hard marching; we passed Sandspruit on the Pretoria line, which we found undefended. Lees, the Naval A.D.C., here came up and told Captain Jones that the General wanted him. He rode off in a great hurry, first asking self and Halsey whether our small commandos wanted to stop or go off. We both replied "Stop, and see it out." Captain Jones came back to say that the *Forte* men and the Natal Naval Volunteers were to be withdrawn, and the 4.7 guns to be turned over to the military; we are to remain. He did not seem to know whether to be glad or sorry but told us that Admiral Harris had wired to the Commander-in-Chief that he wanted the *Forte* men for an expedition up the Gambia on the west coast. Such is the Naval Service, here one day and off the next.

Friday, 22nd June.—The 11th Brigade and Naval guns marched off at 9 a.m., leaving myself with the 18th Hussars, Dorsets, 13th Battery R.A. and so on, to defend Sandspruit Bridge. I was very sorry to say good-bye to Captain Jones and all, especially Hunt, Steel and Anderton, after our seven months' campaigning and hardships together, and I feel quite lonely. General Hildyard introduced me to General Brocklehurst who commands here. We selected gun positions and got the 37th Company R.E. to make two emplacements for my guns. I had a look at the bridge at which the Boers had fired gun shots to carry an important trestle away, but they did but slight damage.

Saturday, 23rd June.—Rode about all day looking at the defences with our Brigade Major (Wyndham), selecting positions and giving my opinion on some of them. Was asked to lunch with General Brocklehurst and Staff (Wyndham of the Lancers, Corbett of the 2nd Life Guards, and Crichton of the Blues) and had tea with them as well—all a very nice lot. Trains are running through to Standerton where the Commander-in-Chief and General Clery are at present.

Sunday, 24th June.—A quiet and cold day. Called on the Dorsets and found that Colonel Cecil Law is a cousin, and very nice and kind.

Monday, 25th June.—A hard frost and heavy mist. General Brocklehurst moved out with the 11th Hussars, two guns of the 13th Battery, my own guns, and a Company of the Dorsets, against some Boers who had been often sniping us and our guides from the Amersfoort Road. We got into position about 2 p.m., and had a small action lasting till dark; my guns clearing the ridges on the right at 4,500 yards with shrapnel, while the Hussars and guns advanced over a high ridge in front. Here the Boers resisted and retired, but on our drawing off into camp later on, to save the daylight, they came after us in full force and we had a small sort of action with lots of firing; we gave them fifty shrapnel. The General seemed pleased with our shooting. Trekked back to camp and dined with Colonel Law and the Dorsets who fed us up right well. Sent General Brocklehurst and his A.D.C. some damaged and fired brass cartridge cases which they wanted as a memento.

Thursday, 28th June.—About 2 p.m. a Flying Column from Volksrust passed through here to follow up the Boers at Amersfoort. This war certainly seems likely to last a long time.

Friday, 29th June.—To-day General Talbot Coke with a Flying Column moved out at 8 a.m. supported by the 18th Hussars and some of our guns, but he had to fall back in face of a superior force of 2,000 Boers and 6 guns against him. We had some twenty casualties.

Saturday, 30th June.—I have been for some days sick and ill with jaundice, arising from exposure and hard work, but am anxious not to give in. To-day I am advised however to do so, and to-morrow may see the last of me here as I go into hospital, and here I may say I remained till the 5th July when I was able to get up although as weak as a rat. I was advised by the doctor to run down to Durban to the warmer climate, so as I felt too weak to do anything else I had to ask the General for sixteen days' leave which he gave me. Thus on the 6th July after giving over my guns to Lieutenant Clutterbuck, I left Sandspruit in an empty open truck at 4 p.m., got down to Volksrust at dark, and met Reeves, R.S.O., who had had jaundice and who offered me a bed in his office, which I was delighted to have; also met again Captain Patch, R.A. We all dined together at the station and wasn't I ravenous! We all came to the conclusion that we were rather sick of campaigning if accompanied by jaundice and other ills of the flesh.

Saturday, 7th July.—At 8.30 a.m. went on by train to Ladysmith which I reached at 8 p.m., and got into Durban the next morning at 9 a.m. A lovely morning and a nice country covered with pretty gardens and flowers—such a change from that awfully dried up Northern Natal. I secured a room at the Marine Hotel, feeling ill and glad to get sleep and oblivion for a time.

Wednesday, 11th July.—The weather at Durban is lovely and I am already feeling better. Have met Nugent of the *Thetis* and Major Brazier Creagh, also down with jaundice. My letters have lately all gone wrong, but to-day I received a batch to my great delight.

And now I must perforce close this record of personal experiences, written perhaps more to amuse and satisfy myself than for the perusal of others; more especially as this being a personal Diary I have been obliged by force of circumstances to use the pronoun "I" more than I would otherwise wish. The war seems played out so far as one can judge. It appears to be becoming now a guerilla warfare of small actions and runaway fights at long ranges; these furnish of course no new experiences or discoveries to Naval gunners; in fact, the sameness of them is depressing, and what with marching, fighting, poor living, dysentery, and jaundice, I humbly confess that my martial zeal is at a much lower ebb than it was a year ago. Yet time may produce many changes and surprises, and I may yet find myself again at the front; who knows!

*   *   *   *   *

Thursday, 26th July.—The quick return to health which the change to the warmth of Durban effected made me only too glad to get back to the front again with the object of "being in at the death." I travelled up as far as Ingogo with Captain Reed, R.A. (now a V.C.); thence on to Sandspruit, and on again in a Scotch cart, which Major Carney, R.A., M.C., lent me, to Grass Kop, a hill six miles off the station and some 6,000 feet high. Ugh! I shall never forget the drive and the jolting, and the sudden cold after Durban weather. Still I was able to rejoin my guns before dark, and to receive them over from Lieutenant Clutterbuck who had been sent to relieve me when I was obliged to leave the front. He fortunately had a share in taking this hill with the Dorsets when in command of my guns. With a whole battalion at first of Dorsets under Colonel Law (who had dug marvellous good trenches), and later on with three Companies of the South Lancashires, and after that two Companies of the Queen's (note the descending scale of numbers), we defend this position, monarchs of all we survey, and therefore bagging all we can get, not only of the numerous guinea fowl, partridge, and spring buck dwelling on its sides and in its ravines, but also, it must be confessed, of the tamer and tougher bipeds from surrounding farms that were nearly all deserted by their owners. For many weeks we had a great deal of fun in our little shooting expeditions. Major Adams of the Lancashires, a keen sportsman, was always sighting game through his binoculars as he was going on his constant patrols round the defences, and he allowed the rest of us to shoot when able. Thus in the midst of our work we had many a jolly hour in those occasional expeditions close to our lines; one day we made a large bag of geese and started a farmyard just in front of our guns on a small nek, giving our friends the geese a chance of emulating the deeds of their ancestors at the Roman Capitol; for who can tell whether they may not yet save Grass Kop if our friends the Boers are game enough to attack.

Sunday, 12th August.—The gales of wind up here are something awful. This evening as we were toasting the "Grouse" at home, a furious blast blew down and split up my own tent and that of others, although fortunately we had a refuge in the mess-house which the Dorsets had made by digging a deep hole roofed over with tin; here we are fairly comfortable and have stocked this splendid apartment with Boer furniture, including a small organ. Our evenings with the South Lancashires in this mess-house have been as merry as we could make them, and our president, Major Adams, whom we all like, occasionally fires off a tune on the organ which he plays beautifully such as it is. The Volunteers with us are to be seen at all times sitting on the side of the hill surveying the country through their binoculars and watching the movements of the enemy. Marking the interest which this being "able to see" gives men, I sincerely hope that in future wars each company of a regiment or of a battleship may be always supplied with a certain proportion of binoculars, or with small hand telescopes, for possible outpost duty.

Monday, 13th August.—General Hildyard rode up here and expressed himself much pleased with our trenches and defences. I had a talk with him about matters and he does not seem to anticipate a further advance of the 5th Division just yet. However, here we are, and the kop "has a fine healthy air," as the General who was quite blue with cold remarked. Neither my men nor self have had any letters for weeks, which is rather dreary for us; our mails are, no doubt, chasing the Commander-in-Chief at Ermelo. One feels a certain amount of pity for these Boers; they are, owing to their reckless and cunning leaders, in the position of a conquered race, and this position to such a people who are naturally proud, cunning and overbearing must be awful. One notices this much even among the few old men, boys and women who are left on the farms; they display a certain air of dejection and are even cringing till they see that they are not going to be robbed or hurt when their self-confidence soon reasserts itself. There is a typical old Boer farmer and his family living at the foot of Grass Kop; a few presents of coffee and sugar have made this family grateful and quite glad to see us; still one detects the cunning in their nature, and they don't hide for a moment that they wish the English anywhere but in their country. Poor people, they have one good point in their characters which is that they won't hear of anyone running down their President even although he has terribly sold them.

Wednesday, 15th August.—We have now watched two fights round the town of Amersfoort, about eighteen miles north of us. On the 7th General Buller occupied the place and we were all in readiness to defend our right flank if need be, but our friends the Boers bolted to Ermelo instead of coming our way. We were all rather annoyed at Grass Kop, however, to see a Boer laager with a dozen wagons, guns and ambulances inspan at almost the last moment and slip off under the very noses of our Cavalry who were drawn up in force under a long ridge, doing nothing for an hour at least. This is all the more vexing because for a fortnight or more we had sent in accurate reports as to this very laager which a single flank movement of the Cavalry would have easily taken *en bloc*, instead of which they paid no attention to our heliograph from Major Adams to "hurry up and at them." These frontal attacks on towns without flanking movements seem to be absurd, as the enemy and his guns invariably get away under our noses. To-day General Buller occupied Ermelo, but as ill-luck will have it the commandos which split up before him have come south-east and are giving trouble on the Natal border.

Friday, 24th August.—The winter is slipping away, and to-day I am writing in one of those horrible north-west gales of wind which knock our tents into shreds and whirl round us dust as thick as pea-soup. Our kop life is becoming a little monotonous but we manage to get on.

BRINGING IN A BOER PRISONER.

IN CAMP AT GRASS KOP.

With the Naval Brigade in Natal: 1899-1900

ONE OF LIEUT. HALSEY'S NAVAL 12-POUNDERS.

Monday, 27th August.—The Boers have again cut the line and are shelling Ingogo, so we must evidently march on their laager. Down comes the rain in a perfect deluge for three days which is most depressing, more especially as our poor mess-house is full of water from a leaky roof and we have to take our meals with feet cocked up on tin sheets. The South Lancashires have suddenly got the order to move for which we are all very sorry. I presented Major Adams with two old brass cases and two blind 12-pounder shells for the regiment from the Navy detachment, as a memento of our pleasant time with them. We have been very busy making our positions secure from attack in case of accidents with barbed wire, besides sangars and trenches.

Wednesday, 5th September.—Very thick mists up here, and as we hear rumours of attack we have very alert and wakeful nights. A great many movements in our front which only succeed in dispersing the Boer commandos without capturing them. We hear of Lord Roberts' proclamation of the 1st September annexing the Transvaal, and we give three cheers![4]

Wednesday, 12th September.—Not much to record. Lieutenant Halsey, R.N., looking very fit, came to see me yesterday from Standerton, and from what he says we are likely to remain on here for some time longer defending the position which is no doubt an important one. My oxen are well, but some of the men are getting enteric. We have to be on the alert against Kaffirs who prowl up the hill with a view, as we think, of taking a look round on the defences.

Friday, 14th September.—Engaged in writing details of the graves of two of the *Tartar* men who, as the Admiral said in a memo, on the subject, had given their lives for their Queen and country. Apparently the Guild of Loyal Women of South Africa have engaged to look after all the graves of H.M. sailors and soldiers in this country and have written to ask for their position. What a kindness this is, and what a comfort to the poor families in England who cannot come out to do so! The two services must be ever in debt for it. We are all glad to hear that Kruger has bolted from the country viâ Delagoa Bay. But why let him escape?

Sunday, 23rd September.—Still here, with all sorts of news and rumours constantly coming up; Kruger sailing to Europe in a Dutch man-of-war; Botha said to be on the point of surrendering; some 15,000 Boer prisoners in our hands and so on; while at Volksrust the burghers are surrendering at the rate of fifty a day, and here at Sandspruit they are dribbling in by half-dozens for what it is worth. But from now up to 1st October at Grass Kop we have to record "Nothing, nothing, always nothing," although in the outer world we hear of great doings, and of C.I.V.'s, Canadians, Guards, Natal Volunteers, and others all preparing to go home for a well-deserved rest. Our turn must soon come, and I am busy preparing my Ordnance and Transport accounts in view of sudden orders to leave the front. The following circular may be of interest as showing the gifts given for the troops in Natal during these operations by native chiefs and others in that colony.

Circular with Lines of Communication Orders.

No. A 23.

The following gifts of money have been sent from native chiefs, committees, and others in Natal for the benefit of the troops in Natal.

With the Naval Brigade in Natal: 1899-1900

The amounts received for the sick and wounded have been handed over to the principal medical officer, lines of communication, and the other gifts to the officers commanding concerned:

From whom received.	*Date received.*	*Amount.*			*On what account.*
		£	s.	d.	
Ngeeda (of Chief Ndguna's tribe)	7/3/00	7	0	0	1st Manchester Regiment.
Chief Xemuhenm	22/3/00	10	0	0	For troops who defended Ladysmith.
Berlin Mission (New Germany)	22/3/00	8	0	0	For sick and wounded.
Native Christian Communities	28/3/00	15	0	0	For war funds.
Chief Umzingelwa	28/3/00	5	0	0	For relief purposes.
Chief Laduma	30/3/00	8	0	0	For sick and wounded.
Members of Free Church of Scotland Mission (natives)	30/3/00	9	5	6½	" "

With the Naval Brigade in Natal: 1899-1900

Natives of Alexandra Division	3/4/00	7	15	3	For Royal Artillery who fought at Colenso.
Free Church of Scotland (Impolweni natives)	4/4/00	3	17	4	For sick and wounded.
Loyal Dutch round Tugela district	12/4/00	41	7	6	" "
J. H. Kumolo (Lion's River District)	13/4/00	3	18	0	" "
P. M. Majozi	16/5/00	3	0	0	" "
Chief Gayede (Amakabela Tribe)	19/5/00	6	0	0	" "
Chief Ndgungazwe	26/5/00	8	9	10½	" "
Headman Umnxinwa	26/5/00	3	0	0	For Sergeant who led East Surreys at Pieter's Hill.
	15/7/00	0	17	0	
Chief Bambata, of Umvoti	3/6/00	3	0	0	For sick and wounded.

Division	Date				
Chief Christian Lutayi, and Mr. Bryant Cole	5/6/00	9	1	0	" "
Chief Ncwadi	9/6/00	219	6	0	" "
	15/7/00	147	1	6	" "
Chief Mqolombeni	10/6/00	5	0	0	" "
Native Chiefs (Timothy Ogle and Ntemba Ogle)	15/6/00	20	0	0	" "
Chief Mahlube	21/6/00	15	0	0	" "
Chief Nyakana (Mampula Division)	28/6/00	2	0	0	" "
Chief Xegwana	7/7/00	1	10	0	" "

NEWCASTLE,
30th July, 1900.

H. HEATH (*Lieut.-Colonel*),
C.S.O., Lines of Communication.

CHAPTER VIII

Still holding Grass Kop with the Queen's—General Buller leaves for England—Final withdrawal of the Naval Brigade, and our arrival at Durban—Our reception there—I sail for England—Conclusion.

Tuesday, 2nd October.—Grass Kop. Still here with the Queen's and my friends Major Dawson and Lieutenant Poynder. What an odd sort of climate we seem to have in South Africa. Two days ago unbearable heat with rain and thunder, and to-day so cold, with a heavy Scotch mist, as to make one think of the North Pole; so we are shivering in wraps and balaclavas, while occasional N.W. gales lower some of our tents. The partridges seem to have forsaken this hill, so poor "John" the pointer doesn't get enough work to please him; but his master, Major Dawson, when able to prowl about safe from Boer snipers, still downs many a pigeon and guinea fowl which keeps our table going.

Friday, 5th October.—We are all delighted to hear that Lord Roberts is appointed Commander-in-Chief at home; report says that he comes down from Pretoria in a few days to inspect the Natal battlefields and to look at his gallant son's grave at Colenso. I must try and see him if I can. One of our convoys from Vryheid reported to be captured on the 1st by Boers, the Volunteer escort being made prisoners and some killed; this has delayed the return of the Natal Volunteers who were to have been called in for good on that day.

Wednesday, 10th October.—Still we drag on to the inevitable end. The reported capture of a convoy turns out to be only a few wagons escorted by a small party of Volunteers who were unwounded and released after a few days.

This is a great week of anniversaries. Yesterday, the 9th, was that of the insolent Boer Ultimatum of 1899 which brought Kruger and his lot to ruin; to-day and to-morrow a year ago (10th and 11th October), the Boer forces were mobilizing at this very place, Sandspruit; and on the 12th they entered Natal full of bumptious boasting. They were going, as they said, to "eat fish in Durban" within a month, and many of them carried tin cases containing dress suits and new clothes in preparation for that convivial event. And they would have done so except for the fish (sailors) and the women (Highlanders), as they styled us, who, they said, were too much for them, combined I think with the Ladysmith sweet shop, which proved their Scylla with Colenso as their Charybdis.

Major Burrell of the Queen's was up here a few days ago and made a special reconnaissance to Roi Kop under cover of my guns; he told us many amusing stories of his experiences with Boer and foreign prisoners at Paardekop while sweeping up the country round there; one Prussian Major of Artillery had come in from Amersfoort and surrendered, saying he had blown up seven Boer guns just previously by Botha's orders. This German Major, it seems, was a curious type of man; waving his hands airily he would say that foreigners were obliged to come and join the Boers so as to study the art of war which only the English got any chance of doing in their little campaigns; this being so, he said, "Ah, I shall go back to my native land, then six months in a fortress perhaps, after that, *sapristi*, a good military appointment. *Eh bien*! what do you think?" He also said about our taking of Almond's Nek that Erasmus, who was commanding at Laing's Nek, had been told that we were turning his flank and was advised to send ten guns to stop us; he thought a minute and said "No, I will not send guns, it is Sunday and God will stop them." Perhaps the Prussian Major's veracity was not of the highest class, but this yarn if told to General Buller would no doubt interest him, because undoubtedly if the Boers had had ten more guns defending Almond's Nek we should have had considerable more difficulty in taking it. The following Natal Army Orders of 17th July, 1900, will show how considerately we dealt with the Boers and others in the foregoing operations in the matter of paying for supplies.

Supplies Requisitioned, Etc.

The following are the prices fixed to be paid for supplies requisitioned, etc.:

No bills will, however, be paid by supply officers or others until approved by the Director of Supplies.

Receipts will be given in all cases on the authorized form, and duplicates forwarded same day to Director of Supplies. The receipts will show whether the owner is on his farm or on commando.

Oat hay, per 100 bundles		15s. to 18s. according to quality.
Manna hay,	"	10s.
Blue grass,	"	3s.
Straw,	"	7s.
Mealies, per 100 lbs		5s.
Potatoes, per sack of 150 lbs.		10s.
Milk, per bottle		6d.
Eggs, per dozen		1s. to 1s. 3d.
Fowls, each		1s. to 1s. 6d.
Ducks,	"	2s. to 2s. 6d.
Geese,	"	3s. to 3s. 6d.
Turkeys,	"	6s. to 8s.
Butter, per lb.		1s. to 1s. 6d.

Saturday, 13th October.—Many exciting things have crowded themselves into the last few days. The Boers who had slipped away from the Vryheid district are again moving north, and are reported in some force at Waterfal on the Elandsberg, 20° N.E. of us. They are said to have a Pom-pom and two Creusots; it seems to be the Wakkerstroom commando and Swaziland police, some 300 strong; the Ermelo commando has also moved on to the Barberton district. These commandos have been raiding cattle and horses every day, keeping well out of reach of our guns; many rumours of their intent to attack us at Grass Kop have been brought in but we are quite ready for them. This raiding has had the effect of bringing all the Dutch farmers and their sons flying back to their farms to look after their stock; they are highly indignant with the looters, have all surrendered and taken the oath at Volksrust, and ride up here to the foot of the hill every day with many reports and much advice about their former comrades' movements, and how to attack and kill them! Many old Dutch women have come also to the hill in tears over their losses from Boer marauders and say they are starving. All this gives Major Dawson and Lieutenant Poynder, Adjutant of the Queen's, a great deal of work and many walks down the hill to interview these people.

Our Naval camp has been strengthened by building stone sangars round our tents to prevent any risk of the enemy creeping up and sniping us in our sleep; still, with barbed wires round the hill, hung with old tins, and trenches and sangars to protect the position, we feel pretty safe, although the gallant Cowper of the Queen's has gone down with one company to reinforce Sandspruit and we miss him greatly.

To go back a few days, I must now mention that on the 11th October came a wire from Admiral Harris to Halsey telling him to arrange the return of our remnant of Naval Brigade to Natal as soon as possible, our brother officers and men who were with Lord Roberts on the other side having left Pretoria on the 8th and arrived at Simon's Town. This wire, as may be imagined, caused us much joy up here after a year's fighting, and I personally celebrated it with the Queen's by a great dinner on some partridges and pigeons that I had bagged down hill on the 10th.

To cap this telegram I received one forwarded on from Standerton next day: "Admiral, Simon's Town, wires, Burne appointed *Victoria and Albert* Royal Yacht; he should proceed to Durban whence his passage will be arranged." This came as a surprise to me, but at my seniority to serve Her Majesty once more on her yacht, where I was a Sub-Lieutenant in 1894, is a very great honour. I cannot well get away however just yet, as arrangements are being made for the relief of all guns by garrison gunners, and I am intent to "see it out," and indeed I must do so in order to turn over all the ordnance and transport stores and accounts for which I am personally responsible, and which after six months mount up a bit. I expect therefore to leave this hill and the front with our Naval Brigade next week, and then for "England, home, and beauty" once more. I shall hope, when able to do it, to revert to my gunnery line by-and-bye, as it has stood me in good stead in the past.

Monday, 15th October.—Another wire from Halsey, who is at Standerton, telling me he hoped to arrange for our leaving together on the 18th for Durban, so we are busy preparing, and I send off to-day my returns of ox transport, which show that out of 84 oxen we have lost 17 in action and otherwise. Old Scheeper, the Boer farmer at the bottom of our hill, whose son is Assistant Field Cornet with the Wakkerstroom commando, has sold me his crane and is making a cage for it. I shall take it down to Maritzburg and present it to the Governor (Sir Walter Hely-Hutchinson), who has done me kindnesses in two parts of the world. I am also busy packing up my collection of Boer shells and relics of Colenso, Vaal Krantz, Almond's Nek, and Grass Kop. We may yet be attacked before leaving, as Boers were reported about ten miles off last night moving south along the Elandsberg. Sir Redvers Buller passed through Sandspruit on the 14th *en route* for Maritzburg and England, so it is quite on the cards that I may go home in the same ship which will be interesting.

Friday, 19th October.—Still not relieved. The railway line has been cut two nights running between Paardekop and Standerton, and about a mile and a half of it torn up, and this perhaps accounts for the delay. We hear that General Buller has had a great reception at Maritzburg as he deserves and that he goes on to Durban this week; he is undoubtedly the "Saviour of Natal," as they call him. The Governor accepts my Transvaal crane for his garden, so I shall take it down in the cage I am having made for it and leave it *en route* down at Maritzburg.

Saturday, 20th October.—Anniversary of Talana Hill. Sir Redvers Buller arrived to-day in Durban and had a great reception. All the newspapers praise him, and the earlier and difficult days of our rebuffs on the Tugela are wiped out in public opinion by subsequent brilliant successes. The General is, indeed, immensely popular with the army he has led through such difficult country and through so much fighting and marching. Very pleased to meet at Volksrust to-day Captain Fitz Herbert of the South African Light Horse who came out with me in the *Briton* a year ago. He was originally in the Berkshire Regiment, but joined the South African Light Horse at Capetown and was taken prisoner by the Boers at Colenso. His experiences with the Boers for four months as a prisoner were, he tells me, somewhat awful. The first week he was handcuffed and put in the common jail for knocking down an insolent jailer, and he had to live all his time on mealies, with meat only once a week. He shows the marks of all this and is quite grey.

Sunday, 21st October.—A wire at last ordering us to leave on Wednesday for Durban. Off I went, therefore, to Volksrust to close my ordnance accounts with my middy, Mr. Ledgard, from Paardekop, who had met me with his papers. Hard at it since the 15th, turning over stores, making out vouchers, answering wires, and writing reports.

Tuesday, 23rd October.—I gave over my guns here and at Paardekop on Sunday to Lieutenant Campbell and Captain Shepheard, of the Royal Artillery, and to-day we are all busy packing, and doing the thousand and one things one always finds at the last moment to do. As we are off at 7 a.m. to-morrow, to catch the mail train at Sandspruit, the Queen's are giving me a farewell dinner to-night, while Bethune's Horse are dining my men. Rundle, French, and Hildyard are reported to be closing in all round in a circle (this place being the centre), and 5,000 Boers within the circle are being gradually forced slowly in towards us. The many men who come in to surrender report that the main body will be obliged either to surrender or to attack us somewhere to get a position. I wired yesterday to General Hildyard, who is at Blood River, sending my respects to him and his Staff on leaving his command, and I received a very kind reply to-day: "I and my Staff thank you for your message. I am very sorry not to have seen you before you leave, but I hope you will tell your gallant officers and men how much I have appreciated their cheerful and ready assistance while with me during the campaign."

Photo by Knight, Aldershot.

LT.-GEN. SIR H. J. T. HILDYARD, K.C.B.

With the Naval Brigade in Natal: 1899-1900

My men have to-day hoisted a paying-off pennant with a large bunch of flowers at the end of it. This looks very fine and is greatly admired in camp. Much to our surprise we had a little excitement in the afternoon as the Boers round us bagged a patrol of Bethune's Horse, and on coming within shell fire to drive oxen and horses off from Parson's farm, my beloved gun in this position was brought into action by the Garrison Artillery under Lieutenant Campbell (who had taken over from me on the 21st), four shells bursting all round the marauders and scattering them at once.

Later on the Boers sent Bethune's captured men back to Grass Kop, having shot their horses and smashed their rifles before their eyes. Poynder and the Major gave me a big farewell dinner, and we all turned in early this evening expecting an attack during the night, but nothing happened. So next morning, the 24th, we got under way, with our paying-off pennant streaming in the wind from a wagon, after saying good-bye (amid cheers and hand-shakings) to all our kind military comrades and friends at Grass Kop. I was more than sorry to leave the Queen's.[5]

I won't describe the journey down at length; the entraining at Sandspruit and meeting all the rest of the Brigade; the farewells and cheers and "beers" from the Queen's; and the false bottle of whisky handed to Halsey by Colonel Pink, D.S.O., which I could not get him to open on the way down. We saw Reeves, R.S.O., at Charlestown, and many other old friends, and ran through to Durban by 8 a.m. on the 25th. Unluckily, I and the middy were in a carriage from Maritzburg in which we couldn't get a wash, so one's feelings at Durban may be imagined when we got out dirty and tired, and saw a large crowd of officers and the Mayor of Durban and others ready to receive us on the platform. What a welcome they did give us! The speeches, the cheers of the crowd, the marching through the streets, and the breakfast, I leave an abler pen than mine, the *Natal Advertiser*, to describe: sufficient to say, I felt very proud of our men who looked splendid, hard as nails and sunburnt, in fact, *men*; and Halsey surpassed himself when he was suddenly turned on to return thanks to the Mayor in the street, and later on at the breakfast. The witty and appropriate speech also of Colonel Morris, Commandant, will make him to be remembered by the men of the Naval Brigade as the "Wit of Durban," and not the "Villain of Durban," by which title he described himself.

Here is what the *Natal Advertiser* says of the day's proceedings:—

Among the first of the "handy men" who, with their 4.7 guns, went to the front, were those of H.M. ships *Philomel* and *Tartar*. Though in many of the reports H.M.S. *Terrible's* men got the credit of the work done, the duties were equally shared by the two other contingents from the cruisers. On October 29th, twenty-nine men of the *Tartar* left Durban, and on November 11th, thirty-three men and two officers of the *Philomel* were entrained to Chieveley. These men went forward to the relief of Ladysmith, and had to face many hardships and many a stiff fight. To-day the last of them returned from the front. Out of the twenty-nine men of H.M.S. *Tartar* that went forward, only eighteen returned; and out of the thirty-three men and two officers of H.M.S. *Philomel* twenty-three men and two officers came down. These losses speak eloquently of the tasks performed, and the hardships endured. Of those who could not answer the roll-call this morning, some have been killed in action, others died of disease, while a few have been invalided. After the men of the *Powerful*, the *Terrible*, and the Naval Volunteers returned, the *Philomel* and *Tartar* contingents were kept at their posts, and, even on their return they had trouble at Grass Kop and Sandspruit. The officers in charge of the men were Lieutenant Halsey, Lieutenant Burne, and Midshipman Ledgard.

Shortly after 8 o'clock this morning a crowd began to assemble at the Railway Station, awaiting the arrival of the down mail train. On the platform were: the Commandant, Colonel Morris, the Mayor (Mr. J. Nichol), Commander Dundas, of H.M.S. *Philomel*, the Deputy Mayor (Mr. J. Ellis Brown), Lieutenant Belcombe, Mr. W. Cooley, Surgeon Elliott, and Paymaster Pim. About 100 men of H.M.S. *Philomel*, under Sub-Lieutenant Hobson, were drawn up in a double line outside the station. The train was a trifle late in arriving, but as soon as it drew up, the warriors were marched outside. A ringing cheer from a crowd of nearly 1,500 welcomed them as soon as they took up a position and were called to attention.

The Mayor addressed them, and, on behalf of Durban, offered them a hearty welcome back. These men, he said, had been entrusted to go to the front to defend the Colony, and they had done it well. They were among the first in the field and were the last to leave, and he felt sure they had done their duty faithfully, honestly, and well. (Applause.) They might be relied upon to do that in any part of the world, wherever or whenever called upon. They were looked upon as the "handy men," the men who had done the greatest portion of the work during the campaign. They and their guns saved the situation. Even when they were marching down, he understood they had had some fighting. On behalf of Natal, he thanked them for what they had done through these trying times. (Applause.)

Lieutenant Halsey, replying, said that after forty-eight hours in the train it was difficult for them to take a reception like this. The men and officers of the Brigade had done their duty, and would do it again if called upon. (Applause.) They were glad that they had been able to do anything in the fighting line, and they thanked the Mayor for the kind welcome extended to them. He called for three hearty cheers for the Mayor.

The crowd joined in the response, and raised another for "Our Boys." Lieutenant Halsey called for cheers for the Naval Volunteers, who had helped the Brigade so ably during the war.

The concourse of people had now greatly increased, and the Post Office front was thronged. The Brigade were given the word to march, and cheers were raised again and again until the men turned out into West Street. Headed by the Durban Local Volunteers' Band, the *Philomel* and *Tartar* men marched along to the Drill Hall. They were followed by Captain Dundas' piper, two standard bearers, and their comrades of the *Philomel*. At the Drill Hall arms were piled and the men again fell in, the band playing them along to the Princess Café, where they were entertained. The Mayor, the Commandant, Major Taylor, Mr. J. Ellis Brown, and Mr. E. W. Evans received them.

With the Naval Brigade in Natal: 1899-1900

At the order of the Commandant one khaki man sat between two white men, the comrades of the warriors being dressed in their white ducks. At the order of the Town Council Mr. Dunn had provided a most substantial breakfast, to which the men did full justice.

The loyal toast having been duly honoured.

Colonel Morris proposed "Our Guests," and said he did not know why the "villain of Durban" should be called upon to take up this toast, or why the honour of proposing it had been conferred on him. He begged to tell them, for the information of those fellows who had just come down from the front, that he was the "villain of Durban." (Laughter.) He meant that if any of these chaps were out after 11 o'clock at night he would find for them nice accommodation in the Superintendent's cells. There was a long time between 9 a.m. and 11 p.m., and he trusted they would not get into trouble. The villain of the piece had to propose the health of these fellows who had come down from the front. (Cheers.) Now, these Navy fellows, if they could do so well on land, how much better could they not do at sea? (Cheers.) They knew how Jack had fought in the old days of Trafalgar, St. Vincent, and at other great battles, and if they had to fight again they might depend upon it that Jack the "handy man" was just as good to-day as he was then. (Cheers.) Jack had proved himself a splendid fellow ashore, and he wondered what any of the landlubbers would do at sea. (Laughter.) The sea was a ripping good place to look at, but from his point of view he would rather be on land. (Laughter.) Anyway, Jack did not like the land; he preferred to be on sea. Therefore, when at home on the sea Jack would do a hundred times better than he had on shore. (Cheers.) He recommended any people who thought of fighting them on sea to take care what they were going against. He did not believe that the British Navy was to be beaten here or hereafter—(cheers)—and he was positively certain, from what he saw of the Navy when they were at the front, that those who went to look at them would say, "No, we will not play the game with you on the water." He was positively certain that they would all be admirals in time. (Laughter.) That was if they only waited long enough (cheers), and if they did not come across the "villain of Durban" they would be all right. He wished them all thundering good luck, and he was sure that every one of them would grow younger, because he did not believe any naval man grew older. When they got their feet on board again they would feel like chickens. He hoped they would all see the dear old country soon. (Applause.) If they did not see it soon they would see it later on. (Laughter.) Now, if they came across an enemy at sea he knew exactly what would happen, and what they would read in the papers—that the enemy had gone to the bottom of the sea. (Laughter.) He dared say the Navy would be able to respond to the toast. He did not know their capacities for talking, but Jack was never hard up for saying something when he was called upon to do so. Again he wished them jolly good luck. (Cheers.)

All save the guests rose, and led by the Commandant's stentorian voice, sang "They are Jolly Good Fellows."

Chief Petty Officer Munro returned thanks on behalf of his comrades, and said that the reception had been quite unexpected. They had had very hard times, and they had had very good times. They had done what they did willingly—(applause)—and they were ready to do the same thing again for Her Majesty and the Empire, and also to uphold the good old name of the Navy. (Cheers.) He advised the fellows to keep out of the clutches of the Commandant, for from what he saw of him he thought it would be better. (Laughter.) When nearly twelve months ago they landed at Durban, the people were a bit more excited than they were to-day.

Lieutenant Halsey asked the men to drink to the Mayor and Council of Durban. Everybody outside knew, he said, how kindly Durban was looked upon. Durban was one of the best places in the station—(applause)—and it was on account of the wonderful way everything was managed by the Mayor and Council. (Cheers.)

The toast was pledged with enthusiasm, and the Mayor said they were proud to have them here, and to entertain them.

With the Naval Brigade in Natal: 1899-1900

The men then fell in again in Field Street, and marched off to the Point, the Durban Light Infantry Band playing "Just a little bit off the Top" as a march.

The *Philomel* and the hospital ship *Orcana* had been dressed for the occasion, and a number of their comrades assembled at the Passenger Jetty and cheered them on arrival. They were afterwards conveyed to the cruisers.

Among the Navals who returned from the front this morning is a little canine hero, "Jack" the terrier, which has shared their fortunes throughout the war. When they left Durban ten months ago a little fox terrier followed them. While at the front he never left them, although he was not particular with whom he fed or what kind of weather prevailed. The firing of a 4.7 gun did not discourage him, and through the booming of big guns and the rattle of musketry he stuck by his adopters. Through every engagement he went, and has come back bearing an honourable scar on the head—shot by a Mauser bullet. The men, needless to say, idolise the little hero, whose neck is decorated with a large blue ribbon from which is suspended a Transvaal Commemoration Medal.

After inserting this account, there is, perhaps, nothing more to be recorded except to say how grateful we all felt to the Mayor and people of Durban for the kind and indeed magnificent reception they gave us; and we could not but add our thanks to Commander Dundas of the *Philomel*, to whose energy and good will, as senior Naval Officer, the success of the reception was greatly due.

Tuesday, 30th October.—After saying good-bye to many old friends of the *Philomel*, and others, and undergoing lunches and dinners (of which the most amusing and lively one was with Captain Bearcroft of the *Philomel* who led the Naval Brigade under Lord Roberts and whom I was glad to have met before sailing) I got on board the *Tantallon Castle*, finding Commander Dundas on board and coming home in the same mail. We left Durban on a beautiful day, and I was glad to find myself in possession of a large cabin. And so I must end this long and rambling Journal on seeing the last of Natal, merely adding that we had rather a rough passage, after touching at Port Elizabeth, up to Mossel Bay, a most picturesque place on account of the towering peaks and ranges of hills running close to the coast-line. We reached Capetown on the 5th November, and I found Table Mountain and the general view much more striking than I had previously thought. We had to wait here till the 8th November, when we finally bid farewell to South Africa which with every beat of the screw gradually faded from view into the dim shadows of an interesting past.

While the revolving wheel of life bears one on to other scenes and toils, with dear old England looming once more on the horizon, we leave South Africa behind with the problem of the war still unsettled, and with desultory but fierce fighting still going on. But let us hope that the shadows will lift, and that the glory of a rising sun will eventually dim and absorb the sea of blood which has submerged that wonderful and hitherto unfortunate land. The lines from the "Light of Asia"—

"Om Mani padme Hun, The sunrise comes,
The dew-drop slips into the shining sea"—

express, I think, the hope of every British heart for South Africa, as they do that of my own.

CHAPTER IX

Gunnery Results: The 12-pounder Q.-F. Naval gun—Its mounting, sighting, and methods of firing—The Creusot 3" gun and its improvements—Shrapnel fire and the poor results obtained by the Boers—Use of the Clinometer and Mekometer—How to emplace a Q.-F. gun, etc., etc.

A word or two now as to what we with the guns have learnt during the campaign, although I feel that this may be rather a dull, professional sort of chapter except to those interested in guns and gunnery, and that the subject as treated by myself may be open to criticism from others similarly engaged. I may certainly say that it was not for at least three months after our opening fire at the first battle of Colenso (December 15th, 1899) that I personally felt myself as "fairly well up" to the constantly varying conditions of gun positions, gun platforms, enemy's positions, and the ever-changing "light and shade" of the South African climate, against all of which one had to fight to get correct shooting; the last-named of these, viz., "light and shade," being perhaps our greatest bugbear, often throwing one many thousand yards out in judging a range by eye, which gift is, I think, the best a gunner can possess!

Then, too, the Naval guns as they were sent up (owing to the work being pushed at the last moment), some on high wheels and some on low ones, some with drag-shoes opened out and others which wouldn't take the wheels, some with the wires from them to trail plate handles the right length and others much too long, caused (I am talking of the 12-pounders) these guns, instead of forming a level shooting battery, to be each one a study in itself as regarded its shooting powers; and we constantly found one gun shooting, say, three or four hundred yards harder or further than the one next to it although laid to the same range on the sights. This at first sight was rather mystifying, but all these small but important matters above mentioned were not long in being put to rights. On any future occasion such defects will, of course, be avoided from the start by the guns being altogether more strongly mounted on broad-tyred wheels and broad axles of similar height, size and pattern, and, above all, with a strong and uniform system for checking the recoil of the carriage, of which the drag-shoe, as it was fitted and sent up to us, was certainly not capable.

I am rather keen on this question of the best means of checking the recoil of a field carriage. A very strongly made drag-shoe fitted with chains to the centre of gun trail will do very well; and these were, later on in the campaign, fitted by the Ordnance authorities at Maritzburg to new "Percy Scott" carriages, which they sent up to us to replace the original "Percy Scott" carriages, which, as I remarked before, were not strongly enough built, particularly as regards the wheels, to stand any very bad country or a lengthened campaign, in both of which we found ourselves involved. In these remarks, please let no one think that I am running down the 12-pounder carriage for a purpose; not so. I simply wish to point out details that, if more time had been available, would certainly have been avoided in them by their very clever designer, Captain Percy Scott, R.N., to whom the service in general (and I personally) owe a debt of gratitude; for assuredly not a Q.-F. gun, or a single one of us with the batteries, would ever have been landed unless it had been for him and his brains and his determination to have the Royal Navy represented in the campaign, as was their due—being on the spot with what was most wanted, namely, heavy guns.

Here I wish to distinctly state my own opinion, and that also of the many officials and gunners, Naval and Military, with whom I have talked over the matter, *i.e.*, that not only did the Naval guns save Ladysmith, but they also in a great measure helped to save the campaign outside for its relief, and with it Natal. And my opinion now, when the war is nearly over, is only strengthened and confirmed by what I have heard the Boers say of the guns, viz., that they are the only things when using shrapnel that have shaken them much during the fighting, and, considering the country, naturally so. That it was to the Navy and not to the garrison gunners that the original credit has gone, was simply because we were here and they were at home at the start. One is, as regards their gunnery powers, as good as the other, and the garrison gunners earned their laurels later on. Still, I have a great hankering after a gun's crew of "handy men" to beat any crew in this world for all-round service and quick shooting, and I am ready to back my opinion heavily.

Returning from this digression to the subject of recoil, we found that sandbags placed at a certain distance in rear of each wheel not only effectually checked the carriage, but also (a great consideration) ran it out again. This system was used both by the 4.7's and ourselves at the end of the war; and seeing that the guns had only half crews, it was a *most* important saving to men who had perhaps marched ten miles, loaded and off-loaded ammunition, and then had perhaps to fight the guns under a hot sun for hours. To fill and carry the bags, however, is a nuisance, and some better system on the same principle is needed, such as the inclined wedges that I saw by photos the Boers were using in rear of wheels; and I should very much like to see some such system substituted for our present one. I have not seen the hydraulic spade used, perhaps that is the *best*.

To put it briefly, the hastily improvised gun-carriage of the 12-pounders had, on account of this very haste, the following defects:—

(1.) Too weak generally in all parts, particularly wheels and axles, for any long campaign.

(2.) Wheels and axles being a scratch lot, none in any of the batteries were interchangeable, which caused many times later in the campaign when wheels began to give out, much anxiety. Several times we only had guns ready for action or trekking by the "skin of one's teeth," and it must be borne in mind that any new wheels wired-for sometimes took two months to arrive on the very overcrowded railway—a single line.

(3.) The system of checking the recoil of the field carriage was a bad one.

(4.) All the 12-pounders except two were in the first instance sent up without limbers, and therefore had to be limbered up to wagons.

With the Naval Brigade in Natal: 1899-1900

This for practical purposes in the country we had to trek over was absolutely useless and caused endless delays. Eventually we all got limbers built at Maritzburg, and equivalent gun-oxen to drag the guns separately from the wagons.

(5.) The trail of the gun consisted of a solid block of wood some 12 feet long; so that if one laid the gun to any long range (in most over 7,000 yards, I think) the oil cylinder under the gun, on trying to elevate it, would bring-up against this trail and prevent laying. This therefore necessitated digging pits for trails to shoot much over 7,000 yards, which in bad ground often took some considerable time. To obviate this defect would of course be very easy with a steel trail of two side plates, and space for gun and the cylinder between the sides.

(6.) The general idea of all the mountings I saw was narrow axles and high wheels, whereas, for all trekking purposes, it should be broad space between the wheels and low wheels. This was amply proved to us by the number of times the high-wheeled narrow mountings upset on rocky ground, whilst the broad low type went along steadily. The 12-pounder gun itself did its work beautifully, shooting hard and lasting well, and owing to the dry climate of Africa we had no trouble at all to keep the guns clean and all gear in good order.

(7.) Perhaps the most troublesome defect of all was that the gun-carriage had no brake fitted. The gunnery drill-book system of "lash gun wheels" may be at once erased from the book for all practical purposes over any rocky or bad country; it simply, as we soon found, tears the wheels to pieces, and chokes the whole mounting up. An ordinary military Scotch cart brake, or a brake fitted as the trek wagons here have, under the muzzle of the gun on the forepart of the wheels, acts very well, and my bluejackets, although not carpenters, fitted these for me. They are screw-up brakes.

The sighting of the gun (drum and bar system) cannot be beaten, I think. Perhaps a V-shaped notch to give one the centre of the H, or hind sight, might be an improvement, as here personal error often occurs. Lieutenant, now Commander, Ogilvy, R.N., always made his men correct their final sighting of the gun for elevation from about six paces in rear of the trail, and my experience is that this is a small but important matter, especially for fine shooting say at a trench at 5,000 yards, which merely appears to one as a line on the ground. One invariably finds that the gun, with the eye of a man laying close up to the hind sight, is laid slightly short of the object; so this should be noticed in the gunnery drill-book as regards field guns. *Telescopic* sights, the patent, I believe, of Lieutenant-Colonel L. K. Scott, R.E., were sent out and used by us with the 12-pounders to fire on the trenches at Spion Kop and Brakfontein, when fine shooting was required. These sights had the cross wires much too thick, so we substituted cobwebs picked off the bushes and stuck on with torpedo composition, and these did admirably. Still this sight was not altogether a success. The power of the telescope, especially in the rays of the sun, was poor, and it took a man a long time to lay his gun with it, thus further reducing the quick-firing power of the 12-pounder reduced already by the recoiling field carriage. As to the 4.7's, it was found that the ordinary Naval small telescope, fitted on a bar and with light cross wires, could not be beaten as a sight for ranges they had to fire at. It is a very good useful glass, and it was, I believe, used both in Natal and elsewhere right through the campaign, and I unhesitatingly give it the palm.

As to the system of firing and gear used, electric firing was very successful as long as one had the gear for refitting and repairing and an armourer attached to one's guns; this, of course, as the guns became split up into pairs was impossible, and I may say that carting electric batteries (which of necessity for quickness have to be kept charged) in wagons or limbers over rocks and bad roads, and with continual loading and off-loading, becomes a trouble and anxiety to one. So for active service I should certainly recommend that percussion firing should be regarded as the first and principal method to be used with guns on the move, carrying also the electric gear for use if guns are left for any time at fixed spots as guns of position. I may here remark that when firing with electricity from a field carriage the battery has to be placed on the ground, clear of recoil, and therefore the wire leads must be adjusted in length accordingly. I am uncertain whether our other 12-pounders used mostly electric or percussion, but I think on the whole, percussion; and, speaking for myself, I certainly did so after experiencing the disappointments which miss-fires often gave one, when trying to get in a quick shot, say from the line of march, with the electric gear. These "miss-fires" are, moreover, often unavoidable under active service conditions, such as we had with our semi-mobile guns. The guns and connections get sometimes an inch thick in mud or dust and require time to clean, when one has no time to spare: the use of percussion tubes avoids all this.

Before we leave the subject of guns the following description of the French 3" Creusot gun by the *Revue d'Artillerie* will be of interest, viz.:—

South Africa.—The Field Artillery of the Boers consists for the most part of Creusot 3" rapid-firing guns made after the 1895 model. These guns were purchased by the South African Republic during the year 1896.... The gun, which is constructed of forged and tempered steel, has a 3" bore. Its total length is 8 feet and its weight is 726 pounds. The body of the gun consists of three elements:—1. A tube in which the breech piece is fixed. 2. A sleeve covering the tube for a length of 3 feet 6 inches. 3. A chase hoop. The chamber is provided with twenty-four grooves of variable pitch which have a final inclination of 8°.

The system of breech closing is that of the interrupted screw, which presents four sectors, two of them threaded and two plain, so that the breech is opened or closed by a quarter revolution of the screw. The mechanism is of the Schneider system, patented in 1895, and has the advantage of allowing the opening or closing of the breech to be effected by the simple motion of a lever from right to left, or *vice versâ*.

The gun is fired by means of an automatically-cocked percussion apparatus. A safety device prevents any shots from being fired until after the breech is closed.

With the Naval Brigade in Natal: 1899-1900

Photo by Symonds, Portsmouth.

CAPTAIN PERCY SCOTT, C.B., R.N.

The carriage is provided with a hydraulic recoil-cylinder fitted with a spring return. It is also furnished with a "spade," which is placed under the stock at an equal distance from the trail and the axle, and which is of the model that General Engelhardt has adopted for the Russian Artillery.

During a march this spade is turned back and fastened to the stock. The carriage is likewise provided with a road brake, which is to be employed in firing only when the nature of the ground is such that the spade cannot be used.

The gun is placed in a bronze sleeve that carries the brake cylinders and the various other connecting pieces for the return spring and the aiming apparatus.

The hydraulic recoil consists of two cylinders placed laterally and at the height of the axis of the piece.

The axle has the peculiarity that in its centre there is a wide opening in which are placed the cradle and the gun. It is provided with two screw trunnions, around which the pivoting necessary for lateral aiming is effected. This arrangement of the gun with respect to the axle has the effect of greatly diminishing the shocks that firing tends to produce.

Elevation and depression are accomplished by rotating the axle in the wheels of the carriage. This is done by means of a crank which, through an endless screw and pinion, controls a toothed sector attached to the sleeve.

Pointing in direction is done by means of a lever known as a tail piece. Mounted upon the axle there are two small sights, forming a line of aim, that permit of bringing the carriage back in the direction of the target as soon as a shot has been fired. All that the gunner has to do is to give the piece a slight displacement laterally with respect to the carriage by means of a hand-wheel, which turns the gun 2° to one side or the other.

The line of aim is found by a back and front sight arranged upon the right side of the sleeve in which the gun is mounted. The back side permits of aiming while the gun is being loaded. It carries a small oscillating level that indicates the elevation of the gun during rapid firing.

The weight of the carriage, without wheels, is 1,146 lbs. and with wheels, 1,477 lbs.

The ammunition consists of cartridges containing charge and projectile and having a total weight of 19 lbs. The powder employed is of the smokeless kind, designated by the letters B.N. The weight of the charge is 1-¾ lbs. The projectiles are of three kinds—ordinary shells, shrapnel shells, and case shot. The weight of each is the same, say 14-¼ lbs. The shrapnel shells contain 234 balls, weighing 155.8 grains each, and an explosive charge of 3.13 ozs.

As the gun can be pointed at a maximum angle of 20°, and the initial velocity is 1,837 feet, the projectiles can be fired to a distance of 26,248 feet.

The crew necessary to serve the gun consists of six men—a gunner, a man to manœuvre the breech-piece, a man to manœuvre the pointing lever, two men to pass the ammunition, and a man to regulate the fuse. The rapidity of firing can easily be raised to ten shots a minute.

The accuracy of the gun is most remarkable. Upon the occasion of the trials made when the guns were received, the following firing was done: a regulating shot, a first volley of six shots in forty-two seconds, and a second volley of six shots in forty-six seconds.

The fore carriage of the gun and that of the caisson are identical. They carry a chest containing thirty-six cartridges, and are capable of accommodating four men.

The back carriage of the caisson carries two chests like that of the fore carriage.

The total weight of the gun and fore carriage loaded is 3,790 lbs., and that of the caisson 4,330 lbs.

On reading over this description of the French 3" Creusot gun, it seems to me that the kind of axle used with it is first class and should be used in our field carriages for quick-firing guns; it must certainly take the strain of recoil off the centre of the axle, which recoil we found cracked our axles as we used them (once in my own guns) so badly that the whole thing had to be shifted and replaced. Another advantage it has is to lower the whole gun and mounting, and the centre of gravity of the weight of it and carriage, and therefore the gun is much harder to upset on rocky ground or going up steep precipices, as we had to do in Natal. This detail of wheels and axle is, I think, the most important one almost in a field carriage. The axle I mention is one bent down in its centre for about two-thirds of its length.

In regard to the ammunition. The cordite charges in their brass cylinders and zinc-lined boxes did admirably, and the amount of knocking about which the cases and boxes out here stand is marvellous. At one time early in the campaign before Colenso and Ladysmith, a decided variation in shooting of our guns was noticed, and was put down in many cases to the variation of the cordite itself, the brass cases sometimes lying out, in fact, in a powerful sun for hours, while the guns were waiting or in action, and often becoming then too hot to touch. Now, however, I personally don't think that this theory was right but am of opinion that the variation then noticed, and even after in the shooting, was simply due to the varying recoil of guns on different slopes of ground and with indifferent drag-shoes. Royal Artillery officers confirm one in this opinion.

As for the shells, both common and shrapnel, they stood the knocking about well, and I never saw or heard of a single common shell used with 12-pounders not exploding on striking, which speaks well for the base fuse. The shrapnel I am not quite so sure about; one noticed often a great deal of damp collected in the threads of the fuse plug and nose of the shell; owing, I presume, to condensation in their shell boxes under the change of heat and cold. Still they did very well and I think seldom failed to burst when set the right distance. I say the right distance because this at first was a slight puzzle to us, the subject of height in feet above the sea-level of course never having before presented itself to us as altering very considerably the setting of the time fuse; and I don't think that a table of correction for this exists in the Naval Service; at any rate, I have never seen one.

To illustrate this, we found at Spion Kop (about 3,500 feet above the sea-level) that it was necessary to set the time fuse for any given range some 500 yards short to get the shell to burst at all before striking; and on the top of Van Wyk, fronting Botha's Pass (some 6,500 feet above sea-level) I had to allow the fuse 800 to 900 yards short of the range, and similarly at Almond's Nek. This is, I take it, due to the projectile travelling further against a reduced air pressure at any height than it does for the same sighting of the gun at sea-level, for which of course all guns are sighted. I should like to talk to experts regarding this as we are not quite sure about it up here.[6]

Of course this firing from a height gives one therefore some 1,000 yards longer range with shrapnel, say at 6,000 feet up, which is a most important fact to remember in shore fighting, and was well illustrated by the Boer 6" gun at Pougwana Mount (7,000 feet) over Laing's Nek, killing several of our Infantry on Inkwelo (Mount Prospect) at 10,000 yards range; of course this was helped by the height they were up, as well as by their superior double-ringed time fuse which we have picked up on their shrapnel, and which gives them in shrapnel fire a great advantage over any of our guns, which have not got these fuses at present. It is interesting to note that many 4.7 lyddite shells were picked up, or rather dug up, by our own men and others, quite intact—this, of course, was always in soft ground, noticeably near the river (Tugela), and shows that the "direct action fuse" should have been screwed into the nose of the shell, instead of the "delay action fuse" that it had in it for use against thin plates of ships.

Before leaving this subject of the gun and its fittings (12-pounder), I again wish to emphasise the fact of how important is the question of recoil. At one time, in front of Brakfontein with the 8-gun 12-pounder battery, we all dug trail pits and blocked the trails completely up in rear to prevent the guns recoiling at all on the carriage. This most certainly gave a gun thus blocked up over one allowed to recoil on the level an advantage of several hundred yards at an ordinary range of say 6,000 yards; but of course it threw on our weak makeshift wooden trails an undue strain, and after a couple had been smashed had to be given up. Still, although I would never advocate doing this to any field gun (*i.e.*, bringing a gun up short as it shakes the mounting too much) the fact remains that the range or shooting power of the gun may be varied with the recoil in a great degree, and that therefore what I mention about a system to check recoil uniformly and with certainty seems to me to be an important one with our Naval field guns. This fact of increased range, got by blocking up a gun, is useful to remember in many cases, especially in this war when the Boers had the pull of our guns at first, and when it might have been worth while just temporarily disabling one gun, and to get one shot into them and so frighten them off.

The newspaper controversy, very hot at one time, as to whether the Boer guns were better or not than ours, and the ridiculous statements one both read and heard from persons who knew little about the matter, were rather amusing and perhaps a little annoying. I unhesitatingly state that on all occasions the British Naval guns inch for inch outranged and outshot the Boer guns; and that the 4.7 Q.-F. even outranged, by some 2,000 yards, the Boer 6" Creusot. This I saw amply proved, at least to my own satisfaction, at Vaal Krantz, when the Boer 6" gun on about the same level as our 4.7 was, on Signal Hill, vainly tried to reach it and couldn't, whilst our gun was all the time giving them an awful hammering and blew up their magazine.

In one way, and one only, the Boer guns had the advantage over us in shooting, that is, with their shrapnel shell, many of which were fitted with a special long range time fuse (double-ringed); here they certainly overshot us, but failed to make much use of the advantage, as they invariably burst their shrapnel, through incorrect setting of fuse, either too high up in the air to hurt much or else on striking the ground. Another great advantage the Boer guns as a rule possessed was the heights at which they were placed, generally firing down upon our guns and troops. Notwithstanding all this, I say again, that their guns inch for inch were not in the hunt with ours as regards shooting power, nor was this likely or possible seeing the great length of the Naval Q.-F. gun and its much heavier charge.

It must be remembered that Naval guns are solely designed and built for use at sea, or in forts, or against armour; and so to get the necessary muzzle energy, velocity, and penetration, a long gun is required; whereas the Boer gun was essentially a field or heavy land service gun. Their guns up to the 6" being on proper field mountings, and much lighter, shorter in the barrel, and consequently more mobile than ours, while firing a lighter charge; and perhaps in this way only it could be said that they were certainly better and handier than our guns. On the march and trekking up mountains this must have helped them a good deal, and from photos which I saw after the Boers had been driven out of Natal I should certainly say that their heavy guns on the march must have been much easier to move than ours.

To give an idea of the difference in weight between the heavier guns I may quote the following figures; that of the Boer guns I take as I read of them in Military Intelligence books:

Weight.   *Weight.*

British Naval 6" Q.-F. 7 tons 8 gun (wire) cwt.

Boer 6" Creusot gun, 2 tons 10 cwt.

British Naval 4.7 Q.-F. 2 tons 2 wire gun cwt.

From these weights it may be at once noticed that inch for inch there is no comparison between the Boer and British heavy gun as regards range and power of gun itself, consequent on our heavier charges. Taking their 3-½" Creusot Q.-F. guns (15 lbs.) and comparing them with our Elswick Naval 12-pounders I should say that there is little to choose between them, they having the advantage only in their long range fuses for shrapnel shell, which fuses should be issued to ours as soon as possible. One always heard these small French Q.-F. guns alluded to with great awe as the "high velocity" gun of the enemy, but I doubt much if they have one foot per second more mean velocity at ordinary ranges than our Naval 12-pounder, although perhaps they may have more at the muzzle, which is of little account.

To illustrate what small use the Boer gunner made of his advantage over us in long range shrapnel, I should say that it was generally noticed by all in the Natal Field Force how very high up they burst their shell as a rule, and so doing much less damage than they might have done; as Tommy described it, the bullets often came down like a gentle shower of rain and could be caught in the hand and pocketed. This of course, I should say, was the result of faulty setting of their time fuse; probably they did not apply the necessary correction for height above sea-level and so the shell either burst at too high a period of its flight, or else on striking did little damage to us. The front face of this kopje from where I am now writing (Grass Kop at Sandspruit, and 6,000 feet high) is full of holes made by Boer shrapnel shell, burst after striking in the hole dug by the shell itself and leaving all their bullets and pieces buried in these holes. There was no damage done by their heavy shrapnel fire at all when the Dorsets took the hill, and solely because of this faulty setting of the time fuse. We have dug up many of these shells here, and bullets simply strew the ground.

The 12-pounder gun limber, especially made by our Ordnance people from a design supplied by Lieutenant James, R.N., when at Maritzburg in November, was afterwards supplied to all the guns, and none too soon; but we did not get them till Ladysmith was relieved and they were badly wanted all the time. These limbers were very well made and very excellent, fitted to carry forty rounds complete of 12-pounder Q.-F. ammunition which was invariably found by us as sufficient, as a first or ready supply, giving eighty rounds to a pair of guns. More could, however, have been carried if necessary, up to sixty rounds complete on each limber; these limbers were strong, with very good wheels and broad tyres (a great contrast to the wretched little gun wheels we had to get along with at one time) and on them there was room also for gun's crew's great-coats, leather gear, gun telescopes, and other impedimenta, which was most convenient.

One fault in them, I think, might be corrected if again required; *i.e.*, the platform or floor of the limber instead of being built only on the forepart of the axle should extend also behind or on rear side of the axle; by this means the Q.-F. boxes of ammunition may be distributed to balance the weight equally on each side of the axle, and so bring the least weight possible on the necks of the oxen or other draught animals drawing the limber and gun along. This, in a hilly country, is important.

I would here note that when on the march with guns under any conditions, one's men should always be allowed to march light, slinging their rifles on the gun muzzles and putting leather gear with S.A. ammunition, water bottles and days' provisions handy on top of the limbers. The carrying of any of these things only exhausts the men for no object, and when one remembers what heavy work they may have to do on the march at any moment—bringing guns into action, rapid firing and running out the guns, digging pits and trenches, off-loading and loading the Q.-F. ammunition, and keeping up a supply which in South Africa at any rate may be at the bottom of a steep kopje with the gun at the top—one recognises the great advantage gained in giving the men as much latitude as possible, and bringing them into action after a march comparatively fresh. For these reasons I would advocate that a gun limber should be made for any service gun, with the object of allowing a certain amount of extra room for the gun's crew's gear and stores.

In respect to range finding, the mekometer (range finder) as supplied to the Royal Horse Artillery and Royal Artillery and also to every company in a regiment (and which therefore was easy to borrow during the campaign), proved most useful to us in getting ranges roughly. To get a range over 5,000 yards one has to use the double base with this instrument, and ranges may then be found up to 10,000 yards, and, with practised observers, fairly correctly. At any rate it is most useful to have something to start on when you get up into position. This instrument is extremely small and portable and should be supplied to Naval field batteries, and also a certain proportion to the rifle companies for land service; it may be carried slung like a small Kodak camera on one's back. Of course ranges can be very quickly found by shooting one or two shots to find them out, and this was done by our guns a good deal, and necessarily so when in action when one has no time to waste and the objects are moving ones; but I strongly advise anyone who gets his guns into a position where he is likely to stop, such as in defence of a camp, or on top of a kopje defending a railway line, or in position to bombard an enemy's fixed trenches and lines, at once to find his ranges roughly all round to prominent objects by the mekometer, as it gives one added confidence and is invaluable when shooting over the heads of one's own men to cover their attack, which is often a ticklish job and to be successful must be continued up to the very last moment it can be, with safety.

This instrument, the mekometer, together with the clinometer, for setting the gun for elevation independent of the sight arc, and an ordinary spirit-level to place on gun trail to tell which way the wheels or carriage of the gun are inclined on uneven ground (so altering the deflection scale), might in my opinion be supplied to every Naval field battery, heavy or light.[7]

I may mention that the 4.7's and 6" Q.-F. were often fired at elevations which did not even come on the graduated elevation arc, and so the clinometer had to be borrowed from the military and used to lay the guns; it is most useful.

For night firing on shore, as practised by us at Colenso and Spion Kop, guns are laid for required distant object just before dusk. The position of the wheels is accurately marked by pegs and lines, and when the gun is laid the sight is lowered to some white object placed fifty yards in front of gun, on which when dark a lantern may be placed; the elevation is read off either on arc of sight or by clinometer placed on the gun. To keep on firing at this distant object when dark, the gun is run out to same wheel marks every time and laid for same direction by the lantern on the near object, and elevation by clinometer. The C.O.'s of regiments always most kindly put their mekometer and trained observers at our disposal on escorting us up to a position.

A plane table survey, using a mekometer to measure one's base, is pretty easily made to get position of kopjes, trenches, well-defined gun emplacements and their ranges, roughly, but it wants a certain amount of time to do it.

As to the emplacing of a 12-pounder or other Q.-F. gun for attack or defence, all hard and fast rules may, in my opinion, be at once dismissed, the matter entirely depending on the nature of the ground occupied and the direction and extent of fire required. Still I submit the following points as being useful to remember:—

(1.) Carefully select the ground. If on a ridge, hill, or kopje, the emplacement must be over the sky-line either on one slope or the other; take a place where Nature helps you, if possible screened by trees, free of rocks, and with soft ground, dongas, or water round it, so that the enemy's shells will bury themselves and not burst on striking. Of course in South Africa, except on the flat, this could hardly ever be done.

(2.) The best form of emplacement is a gun pit about 1 foot 6 inches deep, according to our experience in Natal, the earth or rock taken out forming a circular parapet 3 feet 6 inches high, and as bulky or thick as ever you like on the front face, the floor of the pit being levelled and a gradual slope made out of it for guns to be moved easily in and out of the pit. The size of the pit should be just enough to allow the gun trail to move round on any arc of training when the gun muzzle is run out over the front face or parapet, and to allow three feet more over and above this for the recoil of the gun in the drag-shoes, so as not to fetch the trail up sharp on recoiling.

A narrow ditch may be dug all round the inside of the parapet to allow the crew to get into it for additional cover, and the ammunition boxes may either be placed in this ditch or a magazine dug and sandbagged over when plenty of time is available. A couple of drainage holes may be required in heavy rains to empty the pits on each side. The circular parapet can be built up any thickness, as just said; it should then be sandbagged over till the required height. If in grassy ground, instead of sandbags put large sods of grass to hide the emplacement and to keep the dust from flying, as sandbags are conspicuous. If neither grass nor sandbags are available, make your Kaffirs or camp followers cow-dung the surface of your parapet instead; this dries, and all dust under muzzle on firing is avoided. I constantly tried this plan and found it very effective.

Of all points this avoidance of dust is the most important, as, unless prevented, it rises in a cloud under the muzzle of the gun at every shot. At long ranges, used by the Boers and ourselves, it was almost impossible to locate a gun firing cordite or other smokeless powder except by this cloud dust. So avoid it at all costs. Make the colour of your emplacement as much like that of the surrounding ground as possible, including your sandbags, if used.

Naval 12-pounder emplaced.

BOER GUN POSITIONS AT COLENSO.

With the Naval Brigade in Natal: 1899-1900

APPENDIX 1

HINTS ON EQUIPMENT AND CLOTHING FOR ACTIVE SERVICE.

As a few hints in regard to an officer's kit for active service may not be unacceptable to some, I offer a few observations on the subject so far as I am able to speak from my own experiences.

Good telescopes are most important articles to have in any land company of soldiers or sailors; they were especially useful in South Africa. The Naval Service long-telescope with its big field is very good and powerful in any light where there is no haze (at or before sunrise or when the sun is low for instance), but when the sun is well up it becomes of little use; and then comes the turn of the smaller telescope as used by all Naval officers on board ship. This is a particularly useful glass, and I myself felt quite lost, late in the campaign, when I unfortunately dropped the top of mine when riding. As to binoculars, we found the Zeiss or Ross's very excellent, and all military officers seemed to use them; but, in my humble opinion, they are not to be compared with a good small telescope.

At the start of the campaign the want of good telescopes among the military was most marked, and ours were generally in great request. Many military officers with whom I have talked on the subject agree with me in thinking that a certain proportion of small telescopes should be supplied, say two for every company in a regiment, for the use of those on outpost and look-out duties. It is astonishing to see the added interest which any man placed on these duties shows when he can really make out for himself advancing objects and enemy's positions without being entirely dependent on their officers to tell them. A good glass will render reports from these men reliable and valuable, instead of, as they often are, mere guesswork. At Grass Kop, where we had one Volunteer Company all armed with binoculars which were presented to them on leaving England (with the South Lancashires), the hill was always lined with look-out men on their own account; so interested were they in the matter.

Our water supply, as at first run, with one water-cart to the whole Naval Brigade, was inadequate; but later on each unit with guns got, as they should have, their own water-cart, or else made them with a cask fixed upon axle wheels, which we were obliged to do for a long time. Transport for these was either mule or ox; the former, quickest and best. A field filter for each unit should be supplied if possible.[8]

A few remarks may not here be out of place as to the best fighting kit to have ready for an officer who wishes to be comfortable, and also perhaps at certain times smart, when stationary in a standing camp for some time or on lines of communication. Needless to say that when actually marching or fighting one wears anything and everything that first comes to hand. Khaki has certainly done us very well; twill at first during the heat, and serge or cord later on when the cold came on; but it is well to avoid khaki twill in cold weather as it becomes clammy and uncomfortable. Personally I should say that a serge or cord, thin for heat and thick for cold weather, is much the best for general wear.

I started the campaign with two pairs of khaki twill riding breeches and two serge tunics (thin); these supplemented by a thick pair of khaki riding cord breeches that I got made at Durban when the cold came on, lasted me well through the campaign. For camp wear one can always use the ordinary twill or serge trousers, as served out from time to time by the Ordnance to all hands if required. On one's legs one should wear ordinary brown leather or canvas riding gaiters, only *not* the Naval Service gaiters, as they are of no use for hard work or much riding. Many of us wore putties, and the men all did, but I don't like them myself as they are too hot in hot weather and make one's legs sore in cold.

Riding breeches should be strapped inside the knee and doubled, and perhaps to lace up at the knee would be more comfortable than buttoning. Here I should mention that all the Naval officers commanding guns were mounted, and eventually all got mounts in some way; so riding plays a great part and is absolutely necessary if one wishes to be useful.

I also had two pairs of strong brown boots (an emphasis on the brown), they are far the best; and the soles should be protected with small nails carefully put in so as not to hurt one's feet. A pair of rubber-soled shoes for scouting, sporting, or camp work, and a pair of warm slippers to sleep in are indispensable. Long rubber or sea-boots, on account of their weight and bulk, are a nuisance. When it rained in South Africa it so quickly dried up that we found rubber shoes quite good enough for everything.

It is useful to take three flannel shirts, and under-clothing in proportion; cholera belts also become necessary to most of us I am afraid, and are very important; it is also advisable to have plenty of socks and to change them frequently. Light silk neck-scarves are most useful and prevent sunburnt necks; and in the cold and bitter winds we experienced, and when sleeping in the open at night with heavy frosts, Balaclavas, woollen comforters, Tam-o'-shanters, and Jaeger gloves are highly desirable. Thanks to our kind friends at home we were loaded with these articles during the campaign and found them invaluable.

In the hat line our bluejackets' straw hats, smartly covered with khaki twill and with cap ribbon, did very well for the sun and are nice and shady; they also last a long time when covered well, or even when painted khaki colour which stiffens and preserves them. I found my helmet also useful till I lost it. It is as well to take one Service cap with khaki covers, and a squash hat of gray or khaki; these latter are most comfortable and everybody wore them in camp; but I found that they don't keep out the sun enough during the day, they stow very close however, and can always be worn if one loses or smashes one's other hats.

As to bedclothes, this is a most important matter in the freezing cold. I advise a Wolseley valise to be got at the Army and Navy Stores, with mattress and pillow and Jaeger bag inside; one should have over one at night the two Service blankets allowed, and one's great-coat. Unless one sleeps on a stretcher, which can't be always got, it is well to cut long grass and put it under the valise in the cold weather, as it makes a wonderful difference on the frozen ground and gives one a good night as a rule.

If there are means of transport, it is as well to carry a Wolseley kit bag to hold one's clothes and boots, etc. I think that every officer in this war had these two things, the kit bag and valise, although of course a great deal may be rolled up and carried in the valise only and the bag left behind if it comes to a pinch.

The following articles are most useful to carry always, viz.:—Service telescope, and also binoculars as well if one can afford it (Zeiss or Ross's); a knife with all implements (especially corkscrew); a light tin cylinder to hold charts, plans, intelligence maps, and private maps or sketches; also writing materials, diary and order books, can be carried in a flat waterproof sponge bag case. As luxuries which can be done without:—A collapsible india-rubber bath basin and waterproof sheet, very compact as got at the Army and Navy Stores; a small mincing machine (the only means of digesting a trek ox), and sparklet bottle and sparklets are very handy. Such other luxuries as cigars, cigarettes, pipes, etc., can always be stowed in some corner of the valise or bag. Carry brown leather polish, dubbing, and laces.

Leather gear as carried on one's back should be a "Sam Brown Belt" of the single cross strap kind, in preference to the Naval Service gear. On this one can carry one's revolver, water-bottle, and haversack, which with glasses slung over all and separately, complete all one requires as a gunner. Swords were not carried during this war by officers, as in cases where the rifle was substituted, they only proved an incumbrance. A stick for the marching officer, like "Chinese Gordon" had, cannot be beaten.

A hint as to food before we part. Don't go on the principle "because I am campaigning I must resign myself to feed badly on what I can pick up and on what my stomach is entirely unaccustomed to." There was never a greater mistake. On the contrary, feed yourself and those under you on the best, sparing no expense, and when you can get wine instead of muddy water, drink it to keep you going and your blood in good order. Do yourself as well as you can, is my advice and experience, after perhaps rather thinking and going the other way at first. It simply means that when others run down and go sick with dysentery, fever and other ills, you are still going strong and fit for work. Naturally advice on this point is entirely dependent on means of transport; but when this exists, as it did with the Naval Brigade who had ammunition wagons, a hundred pounds weight or so makes little difference to them if not already overloaded. Take the best advantage, therefore, of it that you can within reason, and up to a certain extent, there being of course always a limit to all good things.

Tents are a great and important feature in any long campaign. I don't hesitate to say that the single canvas bell tent as supplied to the British Forces, should be at once converted into double canvas tents. In the many long sweltering days when the Natal Field Force before Colenso, and later at Elandslaagte, were forced to lie doing nothing, the heat of the sun coming through the tent was very bad; one was always obliged to wear a helmet inside one's tent; and I think in the men's tents (ours with, say, ten in them, and the military who had, I am told, up to fifteen in one tent) the state of things was abominably unhealthy under the blazing South African sun, and I am persuaded that half the sickness among the forces was due to this insufficient protection from the sun. The double canvas bell tent with air space in between the two parts does very well, in both keeping heat and cold off. The Indian tents, of khaki canvas, double and generally square-shaped, are much the best ones we saw on the Natal side and should be used generally in the Army; the extra expense would be saved in the end by prevention of fever and sunstroke.

My own experience (when I and three other officers lay in a field hospital outside Ladysmith just after the relief, in a single bell tent, and saw Tommies all around us crowded into these tents with fever and dysentery, whereby all our cases, I am sure, were made much worse by the torturing sun which poured in all day on our heads), makes me very glad that the "Hospital Commission" is now sitting, and I sincerely hope that such absurd mistakes will be noticed and corrected by them for the good of the whole British Forces.

Regarding the Mauser rifle, as compared with the Lee-Metford, I personally have little experience, but I can only say that the Mauser to hold and carry is much the better balanced of the two, and that the fine sighting is superior. Also some military officers seem to say it is a better shooter at long ranges, and its magazine action is far quicker and superior.[9] Revolvers, as far as I know, have had no test at all in this war. The cavalry carbine, I believe, is universally condemned by all cavalry officers out here, and is doomed to go I hope, being, if used against foes with modern weapons, only waste lumber.

I believe that I am right in saying that pouches for carrying the rifle ammunition are universally condemned in favour of a bandolier, with flaps over every ten cartridges or so. In our Naval bandoliers the want of these flaps was especially noticeable, and the wastage of ammunition dropped out was, I am sure, excessive, besides leaving loose ammunition lying about for Boer or Kaffir to pick up, as they are reported to be doing. The web bandolier is lighter than the leather, and better, so I recommend it, if fitted with flaps, to the notice of the Naval authorities.

With the Naval Brigade in Natal: 1899-1900

APPENDIX II

EXTRACTS FROM SOME OF THE DESPATCHES, REPORTS, AND TELEGRAMS, REGARDING OPERATIONS MENTIONED IN THIS JOURNAL

[*London Gazette*, January 26th, 1900.]

From General Sir Redvers Buller, V.C., G.C.B.

Chieveley Camp,
[*Extract.*]December 17th, 1899.

I enclose a reconnaissance sketch of the Colenso position. All visible defences had been shelled by eight naval guns on the 13th and 14th. During all this time and throughout the day, the two 4.7 and four 12-pounder Naval guns of the Naval Brigade and Durban Naval Volunteers, under Captain E. P. Jones, R.N., were being admirably served, and succeeded in silencing every one of the enemy's guns they could locate.

[*London Gazette*, March 30th, 1900.]

From Captain E. P. Jones, R.N., Commanding Naval Brigade.

Chieveley Camp,
[*Extract.*]December 16th, 1899.

The whole force under Sir Redvers Buller advanced at 4 a.m. yesterday, intending to take the positions of the enemy on the other side of the Tugela. The Brigade under my command was disposed as follows:—Two 4.7 guns and four 12-pounders which were on the outpost line in a position 10,000 yards from the main works of the enemy, from which place we had been shelling them on the previous day, advanced to a small rise about 5,000 yards from the entrenched hills across the Tugela. Six 12-pounders under Lieutenant Ogilvy with Lieutenant James of H.M.S. *Tartar* and Lieutenant Deas of

With the Naval Brigade in Natal: 1899-1900

Philomel were attached to the Field Artillery under Colonel Long. Two 12-pounders under Lieutenant Burne held the kopje from which we advanced.

[*London Gazette*, March 12th, 1901.]

From Captain Jones, R.N., Commanding Naval Brigade, Natal.

Naval Camp, Spearmans Hill,
[*Extract.*]February 8th, 1900.

As to Vaal Krantz, the Naval guns were disposed as follows: ... Two 12-pounders with Lieutenant Burne on the plateau between this hill and the river. At daylight on the 6th, Lieutenant Burne's two guns were moved to a position at the east of Zwartz Kop.

February 18th, 1900. Lieutenant Burne with two 12-pounder guns was left with General Warren at Spearmans and marched on the 10th to Springfield Bridge where he remains under Colonel Burn-Murdoch.

From General Sir R. Buller to Admiral Sir R. Harris, March 5th, 1900. "I much appreciate your congratulations. I can hardly tell you how much of our successes are due to the Navy: their gunnery was admirable."

Report from Lieutenant Burne, R.N., February 16th, 1900, enclosed in letter of March 28th, 1900, from the Commander-in-Chief, Cape of Good Hope Station.

Report from Lieutenant Burne, R.N.

Springfield Camp,
February 16th, 1900.

I have the honour to report as follows:—

Since being detached from Lieutenant Ogilvy's command I moved back across the Tugela river from the advanced kopjes on February

With the Naval Brigade in Natal: 1899-1900

1st. On Sunday, February 4th, I learnt that I was attached to Sir Charles Warren's Division, and received my orders from him personally on that day on Gun Plateau, regarding the next day's operations; I also interviewed yourself on that day in reply to signal received. On Monday, 5th, my guns were shelling the enemy incessantly all day in conjunction with the feint on the left, and in reply to a Boer 3" Creusot and two Maxim Vickers 1-¼ lbs. I received many directions from both General Warren and General Talbot-Coke, as to points they wished shelled, and at the end of the day had expended 250 common and shrapnel shell. At 8 p.m. I received orders from General Warren to march at daybreak on Tuesday, and join the Commander-in-Chief at the fort of Zwartz Kop; this I did, and though delayed on the hill by wagons and by the 7th Battery R.F.A. coming up, and later, by streams of ambulance in the narrow road close to Zwartz Kop, I arrived and reported my guns to General Buller about 8 a.m., at the foot of the kopje. He told me to bring my guns into action, and help to silence the Boer 6" Creusot, and, if possible, the 3" Creusot, which were firing from Spion Kop (position 2) at our field batteries.

As I came into action, and was aiming my right gun at the Boer 6", a shell from it struck twenty yards in front, and covering us with dirt, jumped over our heads without exploding; the shell was plainly visible in the air to me on coming down, and I saw it strike on its side and the fuse break off. The shell was picked up intact at my wagons which were just coming up, by Edward House, A.B., and we have it now. I concentrated my fire on the 6" gun at 6,400 yards, and in an hour it was silenced for the rest of the day; this, of course, was effected in conjunction with the fire from the 5" guns just in front of me, and from one 4.7 on Signal Hill.

During the day my guns also drove back at least two Boer field guns at 6,500 yards, which had been brought down into Vaal Krantz, and which tried to find our range but just fell short; they shifted position, but were finally driven over the sky-line. There was also a 1-¼ lb. Pom-pom in a donga in the valley, which we silenced many times, and at the end of the day had fired some 230 rounds.

On Wednesday, February 7th, we commenced again at daylight; the 6" opened a heavy fire on one pontoon (No. 3), and on the field batteries in front of us, which had been pushed forward there before daybreak. My fire was directed solely at the big gun; my No. 2 standing by and firing directly he saw it appear. During the day my ammunition supply was kept up by direct communication by orderly with the column under Major Findlay. In the forenoon the Boer field guns were brought down again in the valley, and shelled the pontoon, Krantz Kop, and us; they were driven off in an hour or so, but recommenced again later.

In the afternoon, more field guns and Pom-poms on the burnt kopjes to the left of us opened a heavy fire on Krantz Kop, but were driven off by our guns, the howitzer battery (100 yards in our rear), and by the Naval guns on Zwartz Kop.

About 5 p.m. the fire from the Boer 100-pounder was very heavy, and came all round us, the Staff, and Infantry in reserve, and twice my crews only escaped by lying down. Just at that moment I got the order from Colonel Parsons, R.A., to withdraw my guns by moonlight, and cover our retirement on Gun Plateau. This was done, but the steep hill being jammed with traffic, I did not get up to my old position on Gun Plateau till next morning, when I reported to General Warren.

Between February 8th and 9th, I assisted to cover the retirement of our troops over the Tugela, and on the 9th was withdrawn at 11 a.m., and arrived at Springfield Bridge at 3 p.m.

On February 10th, by order of Colonel Burn-Murdoch (1st Dragoons) and the Camp Commandant, I placed my guns in the entrenched camp half a mile beyond the bridge, and up to 14th was employed in making gun epaulements and pits, and finding the ranges.

On February 13th, the Boers appearing in force on the kopjes to our left at 9,000 yards, I rode out with Colonel Burn-Murdoch and other Commanding Officers, to reconnoitre, and find gun positions. They sniped at us at 1,600 to 2,000 yards, and at the advanced Cavalry pickets all night, but next morning, the 14th, after "A" Battery Royal Horse Artillery and my guns had been pushed forward, they were found to have retreated altogether, and we surmised them to be a commando of Free State Boers returning to the Free State.

To-day, the 16th, we received news of General French's relief of Kimberley. All quiet in this neighbourhood.

At present I have 500 rounds of ammunition with me, and 300, in reserve, in charge of the officer of the ammunition column here.

I will conclude by saying that I have nothing but praise for the conduct and hard work performed by my men during the last ten days, especially when under fire; their spirit is now excellent. I should specially mention my captains of guns, T. Mitchell, 1st class P.O., and J. Mullis, 1st class P.O., for their hard work, the latter the best and quickest shot of the two. I must recommend E. A. Harvey, P.O., 2nd class, and leading shipwright, as rendering me most useful and clever work on the gun mountings, etc., and for further designs. Of the rest P. Treherne, A.B.; D. Shepherd, A.B., S.G.T.; Henry House, A.B.; W. Jones, A.B., S.G.T.; Fred Tuck, O.S.; C. Patton, signalman; and W. Dunetal, stoker, deserve special mention. Mr. White, midshipman, has rendered me useful assistance. Mr. Freeman, conductor, has done very well; and the white drivers, McPheeson and Blewitt, excellently. I find the gun teams of eight oxen under the two latter are very useful.

[*The Times*, Thursday, March 1st, 1900.]

The following despatch from General Buller has been received at the War Office:—

Headquarters, Hlangwane Plain,
February 28th, 8.5 a.m.

Finding that the passage of Langewachte Spruit was commanded by strong entrenchments, I reconnoitred for another passage of the

Tugela. One was found for me below the cataract by Colonel Sandbach, Royal Engineers.

On the 25th we commenced making an approach to it, and on the 26th, finding that I could make a practicable approach, I crossed guns and baggage back to the south side of the Tugela, took up the pontoon bridge on the night of the 26th, and relaid it at the new site, which is just below the point marked "cataract."

During all the time the troops had been scattered, crouching under hastily-constructed small stone shelters, and exposed to a galling shell and rifle fire, and throughout maintained the most excellent spirit.

On the 27th General Barton, with two Battalions 6th Brigade and the Royal Dublin Fusiliers, crept about one and a half miles down the banks of river, and, ascending an almost precipitous cliff of about 500 feet, assaulted and carried the top of Pieters Hill.

This hill to a certain extent turned the enemy's left, and the 4th Brigade, under Colonel Norcott, and the 11th Brigade, under Colonel Kitchener, the whole under General Warren, assailed the enemy's main position, which was magnificently carried by the South Lancashire Regiment about sunset.

We took about sixty prisoners and scattered the enemy in all directions.

There seems to be still a considerable body of them left on and under Bulwana Mountain.

Our losses, I hope, are not large. They certainly are much less than they would have been were it not for the admirable manner in which the artillery was served, especially the guns manned by the Royal Navy and the Natal Naval Volunteers.

With the Naval Brigade in Natal: 1899-1900

[*The Times*, Thursday, March 8th, 1900.]

From our Special Correspondent.

Ladysmith,
March 5th.

The following special Army Order has been issued:—

"The relief of Ladysmith unites two forces which have striven with conspicuous gallantry and splendid determination to maintain the honour of their Queen and country. The garrison of Ladysmith for four months held the position against every attack with complete success and endured its privations with admirable fortitude. The relieving force had to make its way through unknown country, across unfordable rivers, and over almost inaccessible heights in the face of a fully-prepared, well-armed tenacious enemy. By the exhibition of the truest courage, which burns steadily besides flashing brilliantly, it accomplished its object, and added a glorious page to our history. Sailors, soldiers, Colonials, and the home-bred have done this, united by one desire, and inspired by one patriotism.

"The General Commanding congratulates both forces on their martial qualities, and thanks them for their determined efforts. He desires to offer his sincere sympathy to the relatives and friends of the good soldiers and gallant comrades who have fallen in the fight.

"BULLER."

From Captain Jones, R.N., Naval Brigade.

Ladysmith,
[*Extract.*]March 10th, 1900.

I enclose reports sent in to me by Lieutenants Ogilvy and Burne, who were mostly detached from me.

.   .   .   .

With the Naval Brigade in Natal: 1899-1900

Enclosure from Lieutenant Burne, R.N.

Colenso,
March 7th, 1900.

Since my last letter dated from Springfield Bridge, I have the honour to report that I left Springfield on February 23rd, marching with the York and Lancaster Regiment to rejoin the main column. We reached Chieveley Camp on the 24th, and I pitched camp on Gun Hill, where I found Lieutenant Drummond and the 6" gun. We remained here till a telegram and written orders were handed me on the night of the 26th, from Lieutenant Drummond, to march at daybreak with the York and Lancaster Regiment to join the 10th Brigade. We marched at 6 a.m. on the 27th, with the Regiment, by Hussar Hill round Hlangwane. Here we found the Commander-in-Chief, who told me, on my reporting the guns, that the 10th Brigade were in Colenso; he added that it was no fault of mine that we had come out of the way, as the orders had not been clear, but told me to cross the Tugela by the Pont as quickly as possible, the pontoon bridge having been removed. At the Pont I had to off-load all my wagons, as the drift below was impassable; and after having got one gun and ox team safely across, the Pont was upset in the middle of the river, and all the work was jammed. During this time there was a heavy shell fire on Colenso Station from a Boer 3" gun, but we were not touched. I had the Pont righted, and my men baled it out before daylight on the 28th, and I took my other gun and two wagons and loads of ammunition across, and hurried on to join General Coke. On the morning of March 1st a body of men rode in from Ladysmith. They proved to be Ladysmith scouts, and brought General Coke his first intimation of the relief of Ladysmith on the previous evening. My guns were in position, and we bivouacked with the troops for some days, but I have now pitched camp and withdrawn the guns. Hearing many rumours here that the Naval men are to return to their ships, I should like to bring to your notice the very excellent service which has been rendered me by my captains of guns, R. Mitchell, P.O., 1st class, and especially G. Mullis, P.O., 1st class, and the clever and hard work of F. Harvey, P.O., 2nd class (leading shipwright), and to mention the following names not before

With the Naval Brigade in Natal: 1899-1900

mentioned:—H. House, A.B., F. Long, O.S. (bugler), S. Ratcliffe, O.S., and to state my appreciation of the work done by all.

[*The Times* of April 16th, 1900.]

Extract from "Times" Natal Military Correspondent, dated March 22nd, 1900.

The Naval contingent of the *Powerful* left Ladysmith for England on the 7th, and that of the *Terrible* left to rejoin their ship on the 11th. The 4.7 guns remain in the hands of the Naval gunners of the *Forte*, *Philomel*, and *Tartar*, under Captain Jones of the *Forte*, but most of the 12-pounders have now been handed over to the 4th Mountain Battery. It seems a great pity that the Naval gunners of the *Terrible* could not have been spared to finish the campaign. Three months' practice ashore has made them nearly perfect in the management of their guns, and they themselves would be the first to admit that, at any rate in that part of the gunnery that was not learnt on board ship, such as rapidity of fire under their present altered conditions and mobility, they have improved twofold since they first landed. Their rapidity of fire was wonderful when it is remembered that their carriages are fitted with none of the automatic appliances for returning the gun to the firing position, but have to be dragged back every time by hand, and then carefully adjusted with the wheels at exactly the same level. As regards mobility, they have on at least one occasion—namely Zwartz Kop—taken their guns up a place condemned by the Royal Artillery as impossible. All this experience is now to be made no further use of, and the guns pass into the hands of men who will have to learn it afresh. A great advantage the Naval gunners had over the Royal Artillery was their use of the glass. Besides the telescopic sights used with the big guns, they were provided with a large telescope on a tripod, at which an officer was always seated watching the effect of the shells, and, in the case of an advance the movements of our Infantry as well, and they were never guilty, as the Royal Artillery have been more than once, of firing on our own men. On January 24th, whilst the fighting on the top of Spion Kop was taking place, the Naval guns on Mount Alice were able at a distance of rather over four miles clearly to distinguish our men from the Boers, and shell the latter. Compare this with one instance that came under my personal observation on February 27th. An officer in command of a battery was totally unable to distinguish, with a pair of the field-glasses supplied by Government, at a distance of a little over one mile, between our Infantry charging and the Boers running away. I see that your Cape correspondent has already said that in this campaign, where we are perpetually fighting against an invisible foe, good glasses are of paramount importance to the rifle. They are even more essential to the gunners than to the other branches of the service, and they are in this respect most inadequately supplied.

Speech of the First Lord of the Admiralty (Mr. Goschen) at Royal Academy Banquet, May 5th, 1900.

"I do not propose to dilate on the courage or resourcefulness, or other great qualities of the Naval Brigades. The nation has acclaimed them. The Sovereign with her own lips has testified to their deeds....

"The ships' companies of the *Powerful* and *Terrible* would be sorry if they were to monopolise the public eye, clouding the performances of men from other ships. Many other ships have sent contingents to the front—the *Monarch*, the *Doris*, the *Philomel*, the *Tartar*, the *Forte*—all these ships have sent men who have taken their part in those gallant combats of which we read."

Again at Reception of Naval Brigade (H.M.S. "Powerful") in London, May 7th, 1900.

"With your comrades in other forces of the Queen, by the defence and the relief of Ladysmith you have saved the country from such a disaster as has never fallen the British arms. The defence and relief of Ladysmith will never be forgotten in British history."

With the Naval Brigade in Natal: 1899-1900

[*London Gazette*, March 12th, 1901.]

From Captain Jones, R.N., Naval Brigade.

De Wet's Farm,
[*Extract.*]June 5th, 1900.

"On May 14th, two more 12-pounders under Lieutenant Steele (Lieutenant Burne having had a severe fall from his horse, and being incapacitated) occupied another hill across the river....

"Lieutenant Burne has quite recovered from his injuries and has returned to duty at Glencoe."

From Captain Jones, R.N., Naval Brigade.

Volksrust,
[*Extract.*]June 14th, 1900.

"It became apparent that the hill (Van Wyk) must be held. General Hildyard was out there and decided to hold it, sending back for the rest of the Brigade.

"I arrived back in camp at 4 p.m. and was ordered to start after dark—as the route was exposed to the enemy's fire—and, if possible, to get two 12-pounders (Lieutenant Burne's) up the hill by daylight, and the 4.7's to the bottom. This we did after a most difficult march, arriving at the bottom at 4 a.m. I halted the 4.7's and pushed the 12-pounders up to the top. One arrived at daylight, the other broke a wheel and did not get up to the top till we were able later to get another pair of wheels from a limber and adapt them."

With the Naval Brigade in Natal: 1899-1900

From General Sir Redvers Buller, V.C., G.C.B.

Laing's Nek, Natal,
[*Extract.*]June 19th, 1900.

"On June 5th I directed General Hildyard, who with the 5th Division was encamped at De Wet's farm, to occupy on the 6th the height south of the Botha's Pass Road, marked on the map as Van Wyk.... The ascent of the hill was very difficult, and it was due to the energy of Captain Jones, R.N., and the officers and men of the Naval Brigade that one 12-pounder (Lieutenant Burne) was in position at Van Wyk at daylight. The other 12-pounder lost a wheel in the bad ground.... The Naval guns and the 10th Brigade were brought down from Van Wyk during the night. I may here remark that hard and well as Captain Jones and the men of the Naval Brigade worked during this war, I do not believe they ever had harder work to do or did it more willingly than in getting their guns up and down Van Wyk. They had to work continuously for thirty-six hours...."

From Field-Marshal Lord Roberts, V.C., G.C.B.

Pretoria,
July 10th, 1900.

"I have much pleasure in supporting the recommendations put forward by Sir Redvers Buller on behalf of the Officers and Petty Officers of the Royal Navy."

Report from Lieutenant Burne, R.N.

H.M.S. *Monarch's* (late H.M.S. *Tartar's*) 12-pounder Q.-F. Battery,

Grass Kop, Sandspruit.
October 24th, 1900.

On withdrawal from the front, I wish to forward for the favourable consideration of the Commander-in-Chief, Admiral Sir Robert Harris, K.C.M.G., a short report on detachment of H.M.S. *Monarch's* (late *Tartar's*) men now under my command, and who have served on shore with the Natal Army for over a year. Since my last report to Captain Jones, R.N., the Officer commanding Naval Brigade, on June 16th, after the victory of Almond's Nek, this battery has taken part in the march on Wakkerstroom and its occupation, the defence of Sandspruit and action four miles north of it, with Cavalry and other Artillery, under General Brocklehurst, M.V.O., which was a spirited little affair, and where the battery earned the commendation of the General on the shooting; later, the attack on Grass Kop and its occupation by the Dorsets was covered by these guns and other artillery on July 24th, and drew a heavy shell fire from four Boer Creusot guns in its defence, this battery at that time being led by Lieutenant Clutterbuck, R.N., when I was ill with jaundice, but whom I again relieved on July 27th, and have continued since that date in the defence of Grass Kop. My guns from here covered the right flank of two separate attacks in force on Comersfoort, the first under General Hildyard on July 30th, and the second under Sir Redvers Buller on August 7th, when the town was taken. We have also covered many reconnaissances, and have come into action at long ranges several times against marauding Boers on the plain at the foot of this hill, but hitherto they have not attacked us, as the hill is magnificently entrenched and has been held in turn by the Dorsets, the South Lancashires, and now the Queen's Regiment. The whole of the intelligence from Grass Kop as to movements of the enemy since July 24th up to this date, has been furnished by my look-outs with our long telescope; and this I need scarcely say has been a considerable and arduous duty for the men under the conditions of violent winds, rain, mist, and storms which prevailed up here (a height of 6,500 feet), since we occupied the hill. These wind-storms have destroyed our tents once, sometimes continuing for days, and have caused much discomfort both to ourselves and the troops, and I have lost a good many oxen by exposure and lung sickness. Orders having come for the withdrawal of the Naval Brigade, I can only say I have been well and faithfully served by the Officers and men of the detachment under my command; and during these months have formed a high opinion of their excellence as a battery, under the varying conditions of climate, heights, and positions, they have gone through in Natal, the Orange Colony, and the Transvaal. All these men, in spite of much sickness at times, have stuck to their work with the Natal Army for a year now, and consequently I think, fully deserve any advancement or reward it is possible to give them, and I am sure H.M.S. *Tartar* may be proud of the men representing her during the war. I wish to bring this general opinion of the men of the detachment, which I hold, to the favourable notice of the Commander-in-Chief, and to specially recommend the following for good service rendered with the guns:

- A. L. Munro, C.P.O. and torpedo instructor (late of H.M.S. *Tartar*).

- G. H. Epsley, P.O., 2nd class and captain 1st gun (late of H.M.S. *Tartar*).

- E. Cheeseman, A.B., S.G., and acting captain 2nd gun (late of H.M.S. *Tartar*).

- D. Smith, A.B., S.G.T., gun crew (late of H.M.S. *Tartar*).

- J. Macdonald, A.B., S.G., gun crew (late of H.M.S. *Tartar*).

- G. Baldwin, A.B., S.G., gun crew (late of H.M.S. *Tartar*).

- J. Sawyer, A.B., S.G., gun crew (late of H.M.S. *Tartar*).

- H. Wright, A.B., T.M., gun crew (late of H.M.S. *Tartar*).

For his good services as armourer and work drawing ordnance and transport, stores, money, and in charge of commissariat, I particularly recommend O. A. Hart, armourer's mate, H.M.S. *Tartar* (late), a man thoroughly reliable.

As regards the Officer and six men of H.M.S. *Philomel* attached to my command, three of whom have since been invalided, I must strongly recommend Mr. W. R. Ledgard, midshipman, who since July 28th I have detached, as ordered by G.O.C. 5th Division, in independent command of one gun, first at Opperman's Kraal, and then at

Paardekop; he has carried out this duty with ability and success, and for a young officer I know it has been a trying one.

I also recommend T. Payne, A.B., S.G., H.M.S. *Philomel*, for good service with the guns.

Expressing my gratification at having had the opportunity to command H.M.S. *Tartar's* (now *Monarch's*) Detachment, I have, etc.

APPENDIX III

DIARY OF THE BOER WAR UP TO OCTOBER 25TH, 1900.

1899.

- Oct. 11.—Time fixed by the Boers for compliance with "ultimatum" expired at 5 p.m.

- Oct. 14.—Boers march on Kimberley and Mafeking.

- Oct. 15.—KIMBERLEY ISOLATED.

- Oct. 20.—Boer position on TALANA HILL captured by the British under Symons.

- Oct. 21.—White moves out force under French to eject Boers from ELANDSLAAGTE. Boers routed.

- Oct. 22.—Yule retires from Dundee on Ladysmith *viâ* Beith.

- Oct. 23.—Death of General Symons at Dundee.

- Oct. 30.—General sortie from Ladysmith. Naval guns silence Boer siege artillery.

- Surrender of part of two battalions and a Mountain Battery at Nicholson's Nek.

- Oct. 31.—General Sir Redvers Buller lands at Capetown.

- Nov. 1.—Boers invade Cape Colony.

- Nov. 2.—LADYSMITH ISOLATED.

- Nov. 9.—General attack on Ladysmith repulsed with heavy loss to Boers.

- Nov. 15.—Armoured train wrecked by Boers near Chieveley. Over 100 British troops captured.

- Nov. 19.—Lord Methuen's column for the relief of Kimberley concentrated at Orange River.

- Nov. 23.—Methuen attacks Boers at BELMONT with Guards' Brigade and 9th Brigade. Boers driven from their position.

- Nov. 25.—Methuen attacks Boers in position at Enslin and dislodges them.

- General Sir Redvers Buller arrives in Natal.

- Nov. 28.—Methuen engages 11,000 Boers at MODDER RIVER. Battle lasting all day. Boers evacuate position.

- Nov. 30.—Sixth Division for South Africa notified.

- Dec. 1.—Australian and Canadian Contingents leave Capetown for the front.

- Dec. 10.—Gatacre attempts night attack on STORMBERG, but is surprised and driven back with heavy loss.

- Dec. 11.—Methuen attacks Boer position at MAGERSFONTEIN and is repulsed with heavy loss. General Wauchope killed.

- Dec. 15.—Buller advances from Chieveley against Boer positions near COLENSO. British Force repulsed on Tugela with 1,100 casualties and loss of 12 guns.

- Mobilization of 7th Division ordered.

- Dec. 18.—Lord Roberts appointed Commander-in-Chief in South Africa, with Lord Kitchener as Chief of Staff.

- Dec. 19.—Regulations issued for employment of Yeomanry and Volunteers in South Africa.

- Dec. 20.—Formation of City of London Volunteer Corps for South Africa announced.

1900

- Jan. 6.—Suffolk Regiment loses heavily near Rensburg, over 100 prisoners taken.

- BOER ATTACK ON LADYSMITH REPULSED.

- Jan. 10.—LORD ROBERTS AND LORD KITCHENER ARRIVE AT CAPETOWN.

- Jan. 10.—Forward movement for relief of Ladysmith resumed.

- Jan. 11.—Dundonald seizes pont on Tugela at Potgieter's Drift.

- Jan. 18.—Buller makes SECOND ATTEMPT to relieve Ladysmith. Dundonald having crossed Tugela engages Boers near Acton Homes.

- Crossing of Tugela by Warren and Lyttelton concluded.

- Jan. 21.—Warren attacks Boers' right flank.

- Jan. 23-4.—SPION KOP captured and held during 24th, but evacuated on the night of Jan. 24-25. General Woodgate fatally wounded.

- Jan. 26-7.—Buller's force recrosses the Tugela.

- Feb. 3.—Macdonald with Highland Brigade marches out from Modder River.

- Feb. 5.—Buller's THIRD ATTEMPT to relieve Ladysmith commenced. Lyttelton crosses Tugela, and delivers attack on VAAL KRANTZ, which he captures and occupies.

- Feb. 7.—Vaal Krantz evacuated and British Force withdrawn across the Tugela.

- Feb. 9.—Lord Roberts arrives at Modder River.

- Feb. 11.—French, having been summoned from Southern Frontier, leaves Modder River with Cavalry Division and Horse Artillery.

- Feb. 13.—Lord Roberts at Dekiel's Drift.

- Feb. 15.—Lord Roberts at Jacobsdal.

- RELIEF OF KIMBERLEY.

- Feb. 17.—Rearguard action between Kelly-Kenny and Cronje *en route* to Bloemfontein.

- FOURTH ATTEMPT to relieve Ladysmith.

- Buller presses advance on Monte Christo Hill.

- Feb. 19.—Buller takes Hlangwane Hill.

- Feb. 20.—Boers under Cronje, having laagered near Paardeberg, are bombarded by Lord Roberts.

- Feb. 21.—Fifth Division crosses Tugela.

- Feb. 23.—Buller unsuccessfully attacks Railway Hill.

- Feb. 26.—Buller makes fresh passage of Tugela.

- Feb. 27.—CRONJE SURRENDERS AT PAARDEBERG.

- PIETERS HILL, the main Boer position between Ladysmith and the Tugela, carried by Hildyard.

- Feb. 28.—RELIEF OF LADYSMITH.

- Clements occupies Colesberg.

- Mar. 5.—Gatacre occupies Stormberg.

- Brabant again defeats and pursues Boers.

- Overtures of peace made by Boer Presidents.

- Mar. 6.—Field Force arrives at Carnarvon to quell rising in North-West.

- Mar. 7.—Lord Roberts routs a large force of Boers at Poplar Grove.

- Mar. 10.—Lord Roberts defeats Boers at Driefontein.

- Mar. 11.—Overtures of peace rejected by Lord Salisbury.

- Mar. 13.—Lord Roberts, without further fighting, takes possession of BLOEMFONTEIN. Boers retire on Kroonstad.

- Mar. 27.—DEATH OF GENERAL JOUBERT.

- Mar. 31.—Broadwood attacked at Waterworks. During retirement R.H.A. and convoy entrapped at Koorn Spruit. Six guns lost, 350 casualties.

- April 3.—Detachment of Royal Irish Rifles and Mounted Infantry surrounded near Reddersburg.

- April 7.—Colonel Dalgety isolated near Wepener.

- April 15.—Chermside leaves Reddersburg to relieve Wepener.

- April 25.—Dalgety relieved. Boers retreat northwards, under Botha.

- May 10.—Zand River crossed, Boers rapidly retreating before Lord Roberts's advance.

- May 12.—Lord Roberts enters KROONSTAD without opposition, President Steyn having retired to Heilbron, which he proclaims his new capital.

- Attack on Mafeking repulsed, 108 Boer prisoners, including Commandant Eloff, taken.

- May 13.—Mahon with Mafeking Relief Column repulses attack at Koodoosrand.

- May 15.—Buller occupies Dundee and Glencoe, having driven the Boers from the Biggarsberg.

- Plumer, reinforced by Canadians and Queenslanders from Carrington's Division, joins hands with Mahon.

- May 17-18.—RELIEF OF MAFEKING.

- May 24.—Advance portion of Lord Roberts's force crosses the Vaal near Parys.

- May 28.—ANNEXATION OF ORANGE FREE STATE under name of Orange River Colony formally proclaimed at Bloemfontein.

- May 30.—FLIGHT OF PRESIDENT KRUGER FROM PRETORIA.

- May 31.—BRITISH FLAG HOISTED AT JOHANNESBURG.

- Surrender of 500 Yeomanry at Lindley.

- June 2-4.—Futile negotiations between Buller and Christian Botha for armistice.

- June 5.—OCCUPATION OF PRETORIA.

- June 8.—Hildyard takes Botha's Pass.

- Surrender of 4th Derbyshires at Roodeval.

- June 11.—Stubborn fight at Almond's Nek. Heavy Boer losses.

- June 12.—Boers evacuate Laing's Nek.

- Roberts defeats Botha at DIAMOND HILL, east of Pretoria.

- June 14.—Boer attack on Zand River repulsed.

- July 4.—Roberts and Buller join hands at Vlakfontein.

- Railway to Natal clear.

- July 11.—Surrender of Scots Greys and Lincolns at Uitval Nek.

- July 21.—Advance eastwards towards Komati Poort begins.

- July 30.—SURRENDER OF PRINSLOO and 3,000 Boers to Hunter in Brandwater basin.

- Aug. 16.—Elands River garrison relieved.

- Aug. 25.—Execution of Cordua for conspiracy to kidnap Lord Roberts.

- Aug. 26-7.—Fighting at DALMANUTHA.

- Aug. 30.—British occupy Nooitgedacht and release 2,000 prisoners.

- Sept. 6.—Buller occupies Lydenburg.

- Sept. 11.—KRUGER, FLYING FROM THE TRANSVAAL, takes refuge at Lorenzo Marques.

- Sept. 13.—Proclamation issued by Roberts calling on burghers to surrender.

- French occupies Barberton.

- Sept. 25.—British Force occupies Komati Poort. Many Boers cross Portuguese frontier and surrender to Portuguese.

- Oct. 9.—De Wet driven across the Vaal out of Orange River Colony.

- Oct. 19.—Kruger sails from Lorenzo Marques for Marseilles on Dutch man-of-war.

- Oct. 24.—Buller sails from Capetown for England.

- Oct. 25.—FORMAL ANNEXATION OF SOUTH AFRICAN REPUBLIC, to be styled Transvaal Colony.

APPENDIX IV

THE NAVY AND THE WAR.

A Résumé of Officers and Men mentioned in Despatches for the Operations in Natal.

Extract from "Natal Advertiser."

GENERAL SIR REDVERS BULLER, in his despatches which have just been published with reference to the operations in Natal, calls attention to a number of officers, non-commissioned officers, and men whose services deserve "special mention." He gives thanks to Sir W. Hely-Hutchinson, the Governor of Natal; to Colonel the Hon. A. H. Hime, Prime Minister, and all the members of the Government of the colony. Rear-Admiral Sir R. H. Harris, K.C.M.G., had also been most helpful. Then follows the list of men "especially worthy of consideration":—

Captain Percy Scott, C.B., H.M.S. *Terrible*, has discharged the difficult duties of Commandant of Durban with the greatest tact and ability, and has been most helpful in every way.

Captain E. P. Jones, H.M.S. *Forte*, as senior officer of the Naval Brigade, has earned my most heartfelt thanks. The assistance they have rendered to me has been invaluable; the spirit of their leader was reflected in the men, and at any time, day or night, they were always ready, and their work was excellent.

Commander A. H. Limpus and Lieutenant F. C. A. Ogilvy, H.M.S. *Terrible*, and Lieutenant H. W. James, H.M.S. *Tartar*. These three Officers were indefatigable. There never was a moment in the day that they were not working hard and well to advance the work in hand.

The names of the following officers, warrant officers, non-commissioned officers, and men of the Naval Brigade, Sir Redvers Buller adds, have been brought to his notice for gallant or meritorious services by general officers and officers commanding units:—

OFFICERS—NAVAL BRIGADE.

- Lieutenant C. P. Hunt, H.M.S. *Forte*.

- Lieutenant C. R. N. Burne, H.M.S. *Philomel*.

- Staff-Surgeon F. J. Lilly, H.M.S. *Forte*.

- Surgeon C. C. Macmillan, H.M.S. *Terrible*.

- Surgeon E. C. Lomas, H.M.S. *Terrible*.

- Acting-Gunner J. Wright, H.M.S. *Terrible*.

- Midshipman R. B. Hutchinson, H.M.S. *Terrible*.

- Midshipman H. S. Boldero, H.M.S. *Terrible*.

- Midshipman G. L. Hodson, H.M.S. *Terrible*.

- Clerk W. T. Hollin, H.M.S. *Philomel*.

With the Naval Brigade in Natal: 1899-1900

Photo by Debenham, Southsea.

CAPTAIN E. P. JONES, R.N.

With the Naval Brigade in Natal: 1899-1900

WARRANT, NON-COMMISSIONED OFFICERS, AND MEN.

- Chief Petty Officer T. Baldwin, H.M.S. *Terrible*.
- Chief Petty Officer W. Bate, H.M.S. *Terrible*.
- Chief Petty Officer B. Stephens, H.M.S. *Terrible*.
- First-Class Petty Officer P. Cashman, H.M.S. *Philomel*.
- Second-Class Petty Officer C. Challoner, H.M.S. *Terrible*.
- Second-Class Petty Officer J. J. Frennett, H.M.S. *Philomel*.
- Master-at-Arms G. Crowe, H.M.S. *Terrible*.
- Armourer Ellis, H.M.S. *Terrible*.
- F. Moore, A.B., H.M.S. *Forte*.

THE NAVAL BRIGADE.

General Sir Redvers Buller, in a despatch dated Laing's Nek, June 19th, 1900, says: "I desire to bring to notice the following officer:—

"Captain E. P. Jones, R.N., Naval Brigade.

"It was due to the energy and perseverance of the officers and men alike, following the excellent example set them by their Commander, Captain Jones, that it was possible to place the Naval guns in position on the 8th, and get them forward subsequently in time to accompany the advance on the 10th. The excellent marksmanship of the Naval Brigade, and the skilful distribution of their fire, contributed materially to the successful result of the attack on Allemann's Nek on June 11th."

The following names are mentioned by Commanders as having performed good services, in addition to those previously mentioned:—

- Lieutenant G. P. Hunt, H.M.S. *Forte*.

- Lieutenant F. W. Melvill, H.M.S. *Forte*.

- Lieutenant C. R. N. Burne, H.M.S. *Philomel*.

- Lieutenant A. Halsey, H.M.S. *Philomel*.

- Midshipman W. R. Ledgard, H.M.S. *Philomel*.

- John Restal, chief armourer, H.M.S. *Tartar*.

- Alexander Monro, C.P.O., H.M.S. *Tartar*.

- J. Weatherhead, P.O., H.M.S. *Philomel*.

- E. Waring, yeoman of signals.

Referring to the work at the base and on the lines of communication, General Buller, in the despatch dated ss. *Dunvegan Castle*, November 9th, says:—

"The Naval transport work at Durban has been throughout under the charge of Captain Van Koughnet, R.N. I desire to take this opportunity of bringing to notice the excellent service which he has rendered. Owing to his tact and ability, the difficult and ofttimes very heavy work of embarkations and disembarkations has passed smoothly and well.

"Commander G. E. Holland, D.S.O., Indian Marine, has also been employed at Durban throughout. His genius for organisation, and his knowledge of transport requirements, is, I should say, unrivalled. He undertook the alteration of the transports which were fitted at Durban as hospital ships, and the result of his work has been universally admitted to have been a conspicuous success. I strongly recommend him to your consideration.

"Warrant Officer Carpenter S. J. Lacey, R.N., has rendered valuable service in supervising the fitting of hospital ships and in transport work generally. I recommend him to your favourable notice.

"The following officers acted as my aides-de-camp, and I submit their names for your favourable consideration. Each and all of them are thoroughly capable and deserving officers, and rendered me great assistance:—

"Commander Edgar Lees, Royal Navy (and others).

"Lieutenant A. Halsey, R.N., H.M.S. *Philomel*, commanded the last detachment of the Naval Brigade which was left with the Natal Field Force, and, like all the rest of the Brigade, their services were most valuable."

With the Naval Brigade in Natal: 1899-1900

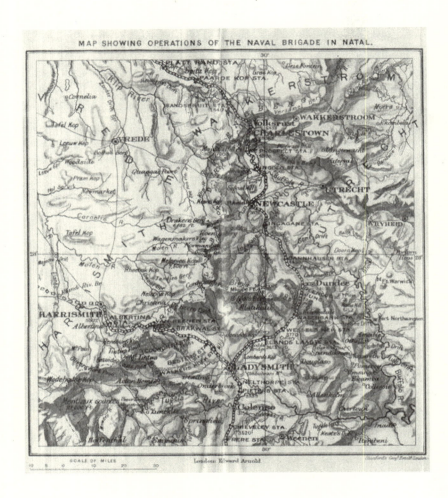

FOOTNOTES

Footnote 1: General Sir Owen Tudor Burne.

Footnote 2: Having lost over 100 officers and men killed and wounded at Venter's Spruit, the 2nd battalion of the regiment went subsequently into action at Spion Kop 800 strong, and only 553 answered the roll call next day.

Footnote 3: The number of killed, wounded, and missing in the Natal Field Force, in the operations thus briefly alluded to, from Colenso (15th December, 1899) to the Relief of Ladysmith (28th February, 1900), amounted to 301 officers and 5,028 men.

Footnote 4: The following is a copy of a telegram which the Governor received from Lord Roberts, dated 13th September, 1900:

"I have ordered the following proclamation to be printed and widely circulated in English and Dutch.

"The late President, with Mr. Reitz, and the archives of the South African Republic, have crossed the Portuguese frontier and arrived at Lourenso Marques, with a view of sailing for Europe at an early date. Mr. Kruger has formally resigned the position he held as President of the South African Republic, thus severing his official connection with the Transvaal.

"Mr. Kruger's action shows how hopeless, in his opinion, is the war which has now been carried on for nearly a year, and his desertion of the Boer cause should make it clear to his fellow-burghers that it is useless for them to continue the struggle any longer.

"It is probably unknown to the inhabitants of the Transvaal and Orange River Colony that nearly 15,000 of their fellow-subjects are now prisoners of war, not one of whom will be released until those now in arms against us surrender unconditionally.

"The burghers must now by this time be cognisant of the fact that no intervention on their behalf will come from any of the Great Powers, and, further, that the British Empire is determined to complete the work which has already cost so many valuable lives, and to carry to its conclusion the war declared against her by the late Governments of the Transvaal and Orange Free State—a war to which there can be but one ending.

"If any further doubts remain in the minds of the burghers as to Her Britannic Majesty's intentions, they should be dispelled by the permanent manner in which the country is gradually being occupied by Her Majesty's forces, and by the issue of the proclamations signed by me on the 24th May and the 1st September, 1900, annexing the Orange Free State and the South African Republic respectively, in the name of Her Majesty.

"I take this opportunity of pointing out that, except in the small area occupied by the Boer army under the personal command of Commandant General Botha, the war is degenerating into operations carried on in an irregular and irresponsible manner by small, and, in very many cases, insignificant bodies of men.

"I should be failing in my duty to Her Majesty's Government and to Her Majesty's Army in South Africa, if I neglected to use every means in my power to bring such irregular warfare to an early conclusion.

"The means which I am compelled to adopt are those which the customs of war prescribe as being applicable to such cases.

"They are ruinous to the country, entail endless suffering on the burghers and their families, and the longer this guerilla warfare continues the more vigorously must they be enforced."

Footnote 5: Poor Poynder! I was dreadfully sorry to hear he died of enteric at Kronstadt just a year after this event; there was never a nicer chap or a better soldier, and it's hard lines losing him.

Footnote 6: I am since glad to hear from Lieutenant Henderson of H.M.S. *Excellent*, that he is engaged in working out a table of corrections, such as I mention, and is also interesting himself in the question of "range-finders," and "filters," and other necessities for naval service.

Footnote 7: Since writing this opinion I think, perhaps, it will be well to pause till the results of Professor George Forbes', F.R.S., experiments with a new stereoscopic instrument in South Africa are to hand; he is there at present by request of Lord Kitchener with his new invention. For full report of this instrument I would refer to Professor Forbes' paper read at the Society of Arts, December 18th, 1901. It is sufficient now to say that the instrument folds up to 3 foot 6 inches in length, can be used by one observer only standing, kneeling, or lying down, has great accuracy and portability, and has received the support of Sir George Clarke and other authorities.

Footnote 8: The proper filtering of water for use in water-bottles and indeed for all drinking purposes, is most important, and especially so in hot weather, when men are always wanting a drink at off times, and will have it of course. Late in the war, the "Berkefeld Field Service Filter" was supplied to us by the Ordnance Department, and is very good; it packs up in what looks like a large-sized luncheon basket, and is very portable; it is simple to look after, if directions are followed, and will make about thirty-four pints in ten minutes, or, enough to fill fifteen men's water-bottles; consequently it can easily be used on the march during short halts, and whenever water is passed to fill up water-bottles, and it is quickly packed up again. For any individual who wishes to carry a filter on his own person, I would recommend a small "Berkefeld Cylinder or porous candle" and small "Pasteur pump" with the necessary rubber tubes; this makes a very small parcel; it would only take up about one quarter of the Service haversack, and is well worth taking I am sure. The "Berkefeld Filter" should be supplied to ships in case of landing Brigades—one to every unit of 100 is the proper proportion as recommended by the firm.

Footnote 9: Since writing this about the Mauser, Captain Cowper of the Queen's tells me that on the whole he considers the Lee-Metford superior, and that the Boers he has met have told him they hold it to be a harder shooter at long ranges. However, it seems to me that the better balance and magazine of the Mauser counteract this and give it the preference.

Breinigsville, PA USA
27 November 2009
228283BV00001B/101/P